D1784027

1 MONTH OF
FREE
READING

at

www.ForgottenBooks.com

By purchasing this book you are eligible for one month membership to ForgottenBooks.com, giving you unlimited access to our entire collection of over 1,000,000 titles via our web site and mobile apps.

To claim your free month visit:
www.forgottenbooks.com/free753232

* Offer is valid for 45 days from date of purchase. Terms and conditions apply.

ISBN 978-0-483-15600-5
PIBN 10753232

This book is a reproduction of an important historical work. Forgotten Books uses
state-of-the-art technology to digitally reconstruct the work, preserving the original format
whilst repairing imperfections present in the aged copy. In rare cases, an imperfection in
the original, such as a blemish or missing page, may be replicated in our edition. We do,
however, repair the vast majority of imperfections successfully; any imperfections that
remain are intentionally left to preserve the state of such historical works.

Forgotten Books is a registered trademark of FB &c Ltd.
Copyright © 2018 FB &c Ltd.
FB &c Ltd, Dalton House, 60 Windsor Avenue, London, SW19 2RR.
Company number 08720141. Registered in England and Wales.

For support please visit www.forgottenbooks.com

THE

PRESENT STATE

OF THE

EUROPEAN SETTLEMENTS

ON THE

MISSISIPPI.

THE

PRESENT STATE

OF THE

EUROPEAN SETTLEMENTS

ON THE

MISSISIPPI;

WITH

A GEOGRAPHICAL DESCRIPTION of that RIVER,

ILLUSTRATED BY

PLANS AND DRAUGHTS.

By Captain PHILIP PITTMAN.

LONDON,

Printed for J. NOURSE, Bookseller to His MAJESTY.

MDCCLXX.

Bar
F352
P68

3236

PREFACE.

THE European settlements on the river Missisippi comprehend Louisiana, part of West Florida, and the country of the Illinois. Five years residence as an engineer in those countries, during which time I was chiefly employed in surveying and exploring their interior parts, and an acquaintance with the principal inhabitants, enables me to speak with at least as much authority as any author who has hitherto wrote on the same subject.

Louisiana is no longer the same as in the time of Pere Hennepin; and all other authors that I have read on this subject rather abound with Indian stories and *talks*, than with useful information.

Father Charlevoix made so rapid a progress through those countries, that the greatest part of what he advances must be from the doubtful information of others, and not from his own personal knowledge. Neither is the reader recompensed by the small quantity of pure ore he can extract from that mass of dross, in the elaborate accounts of Le Page du Pratz.

It may be thought extraordinary that I have confined my accounts to the banks of the Missisippi, and not touched on the other parts of West Florida, which may be supposed equally interesting.

This work was originally wrote at the request, and for the perusal only, of the secretary of state for the colonies;

4   and

and I imagined that he muſt have received every information neceſſary to form a perfect knowledge of that province, from perſons who have commanded in it. Beſides,
my ingenious friend governor Johnſtone has told me, that
he intends ſoon to publiſh a book on this ſubject ; by which
means the deficiency in mine will be amply made up, and
the publick will have the advantage of receiving inſtruction
and entertainment from a much more pleaſing and
abler pen.

I am ſurpriſed that nobody has yet attempted to wipe
off the unfavourable impreſſions that have taken place in
the minds of many people, from the unjuſt reports
made of the climate of Weſt Florida, and which ſtill re-
tards the ſettling of that fine country. A regard for truth,
and a deſire to render ſervice to that valuable province, the
welfare of which has been obſtructed by ignorance and
miſrepreſentation, makes me take this occaſion to ſhew
the true cauſes of its ſuppoſed unhealthineſs.

Penſacola and Mobile have both proved fatal to our
troops ; the former from miſmanagement, the latter from
its ſituation. When we took poſſeſſion of Penſacola, in
the latter end of the year 1763, it conſiſted of a fort and
a few ſtraggling houſes ; the fort was conſtructed of high
ſtockades, encloſing in a very ſmall ſpace a houſe for the
governor, and ſeveral miſerable huts, built with pieces of
bark, covered with the ſame materials, and moſt of
them without floors ; ſo that in the ſummer they were as
hot as ſtoves, and the land engendered all ſorts of ver-
min : in theſe wretched habitations the officers and
ſoldiers dwelt.

After

After we had poffeffion fome time, the commandant, with a view of making the fortification more refpectable, furrounded the fort with a ditch; which, in fact, could anfwer no other purpofe, than holding a quantity of ftagnated water to empoifon the little air that could find its way into the garrifon. The thirty-firft regiment of foot, which fuffered remarkably from ficknefs and mortality in this place, was fent to it in the hotteft part of the fummer of 1765, unprovided with every thing neceffary to preferve health in fuch a fudden change of climate. Brigadier-general Haldimand, in the beginning of 1767, immediately after his arrival here, caufed the enceinte of the fort to be confiderably extended, widened the ftreets, removed every thing that could obftruct a free circulation of air, and laid the place open to the fea, to give admiffion to the breezes. The enfuing fummer was exceffive hot, the thermometer having rofe to one hundred and fourteen degrees; yet, by the falutary precautions the general had taken, the troops were remarkably healthy, few fell fick, and fcarce any died; although their lodgings, which of themfelves may be fuppofed fufficient to deftroy a good conftitution, were little improved: from hence I prefume that Penfacola is as healthy as any Englifh fettlement in the fouthern provinces of North America.

Mobile is fituated on the banks of the river of that name, juft at the place where the frefh and falt waters mix; when the tide goes out it leaves an abundance of fmall fifhes on the marfhes which lie oppofite the town, and the heat of the fun in fummer kills the fifh; and the ftench of them, of the ftagnated water in the neighbouring fwamps, and the flimy mud, render the air putrid. To this

this may be added, that the water of the wells is brackiſh, and there is none to be found wholſome within leſs than one mile and a half of the place. The twenty-firſt regiment of foot was ſent to Mobile at the ſame time that the *thirty-firſt* regiment garriſoned Penſacola, and being equally unprovided with things neceſſary for troops newly arrived from Europe, and unſeaſoned to ſuch a climate, ſuffered almoſt as much. I ſhall only add on this ſubjeſt, which is a little diſtant from the true intent of my preface, that Weſt Florida poſſeſſes the greateſt advantage, as to its ſituation for commerce, and the communications to the different parts are rendered eaſy by fine navigable rivers, the banks of which are covered by a freſh luxuriant ſoil, capable of producing every thing natural to theſe climates.

I have endeavoured to be as conciſe as poſſible ; indeed the purpoſe it was wrote for ſeemed to demand it : I could with eaſe have been much more diffuſe on ſubjeſts in which ſo much matter is contained.

It is with fear and diffidence that I preſume to appear as an author ; but a deſire of communicating what I have been aſſured by friends would be of uſe to the publick, has been my only inducement ; and if they have judged right, my utmoſt wiſhes will be amply gratified.

THE
PRESENT STATE
OF THE
EUROPEAN SETTLEMENTS
On the MISSISIPPI.

Of the River MISSISIPPI.

T H E river Miffifippi has been known by a variety of names; the firft difcoverers from Canada gave it the name of Colbert, in honour to that great minifter, who was then in power. The famous adventurer, Monfieur de Salle, when he difcovered the mouth, called it the river Saint Louis, by which name it has ever been diftinguifhed in all publick acts, refpecting the province of Louiffianna: But its prefent general appellation of Miffifippi is a corruption of *Metchafippi*; by which name it is ftill known to the Northern Savages, that word fignifying, in their language, the Father of Rivers.

Nothing can, with propriety, be afferted with refpect to the fource of this river, tho' there are people ftill exifting, who pretend to have been there. The accounts, which I think fhould be paid moft attention to, are thofe which have been given by the *Sioux*, a

very

very numerous itinerant nation of Indians, who generally reside in the countries North of the Missisippi: A few of them have sometimes come to the French post, on the River Illinois, to barter skins and furrs; but in general they dislike the Europeans, and have little inclination to be much acquainted with them. Their account is as follows: The river Missisippi rises from a very extensive swamp, and its waters are encreased by several rivers (some of them not inconsiderable) emptying themselves into it in its course to the fall of St. Anthony, which, by their accounts, is not less than seven hundred leagues from the great swamps: This is formed by a rock running a-cross the river, and falls about twelve feet perpendicular; and this place is known to be eight hundred leagues from the sea. So that it is most probable that the Missisippi runs, at least, four thousand five hundred miles.

The principal rivers which fall into the Missisippi, below the fall of St. Anthony, are, the river St. Pierre, which comes from the West; Saint Croix, from the East; Moingona, which is two hundred and fifty leagues below the fall, comes from the West, and is said to run one hundred and fifty leagues; and the river Illinois, the source of which is near the lake Michigan, East of the Missisippi two hundred leagues.

The source of the river Missoury is unknown; the French traders go betwixt three and four hundred leagues up, to traffic with the Indians who inhabit near its banks, and this branch of commerce is very considerable; it employs annually eight thousand pounds worth of European goods, including a small quantity of rum, of all which the freight amounts to about one hundred per cent. Their returns are, at least, at the rate of three hundred per cent. so that they are certain of two hundred per cent. profit. The mouth of this great river is five leagues below the river Illinois, and is generally called five hundred from the sea, tho' in fact it is not more than four hundred and fifty. From its confluence to its source is supposed to be

eight

eight hundred leagues, running from the north-weft to the foutheaft. The muddy waters of the Miffoury prevail over thofe of the Miffifippi, running with violent rapidity to the ocean. The Miffifippi glides with a gentle and clear ftream, 'till it meets with this interruption. The next river of note, is the Ohio or Belle Riviere; it empties itfelf about feventy leagues below the Miffoury: its fource is near the lake Erie, running from the north-eaft to the fouth-weft, upwards of four hundred leagues.

Ninety leagues further down is the river Saint Francis, on the weft fide of the Miffifippi: this is a very fmall river, and is remarkable for nothing but being the general rendez-vous of the hunters from New Orleans, who winter there, and make a provifion of falted meats, fuet, and bears oil, for the fupply of that city. The river Arkanfas is thirty-five leagues lower down, and two hundred from New Orleans; it is fo called from a nation of Indians of the fame name; its fource is faid to be in the fame latitude as Santa Fé in New Mexico, and holds its courfe near three hundred leagues.

The river Yazous comes from the north-eaft, and difcharges itfelf into the Miffifippi, fixty leagues from the Arkanfas: formerly a nation of Indians of the fame name had their villages on it, and there was a French poft and fettlement. The nation is entirely extinct, and there is not the leaft trace of any fettlement.

It is near fixty leagues from this little river to the river Rouge; which is fo called from its waters, being of a reddifh colour, and they tinge thofe of the Miffifippi at the time of the floods; its fource is in New Mexico, and it runs about two hundred leagues: the river Noir empties itfelf into this river about ten leagues from its confluence. The famous Ferdinand Soto ended his difcoveries at the entrance of the river Rouge, and was buried there.

Near

Near feventy leagues up this river is a very confiderable poft, be-longing to the French; it is a frontier on the Spanifh fettlements, being twenty miles from the Fort of Adaies. The French fort is garrifoned by a captain, two fubalterns, and about fifty men : there are forty families, confifting moftly of difcharged foldiers, and fome merchants who trade with the Spaniards. A great quantity of to-bacco is cultivated at this port, and fells for a good price at New Orleans, being held in great efteem : they fend alfo fome peltry, which they receive in trade from the neighbouring Indians.

From the river Rouge to the fea, there are only fome fmall brooks, of no account. The Bayouk of Peloufas, which is about three miles from the river Rouge and the river Ibberville, are defcribed in the account hereafter given of the fettlements on the river Mif-fifippi.

It is peculiar to the river Miffifippi, that no part of the waters which overflow its banks, ever return to their former channel : this is a circumftance, which I believe is not to be met with in any other river in the world. All the lands from the river Ibbeville to the fea, have been formed in the fucceffion of ages, by the vaft quantities of flimy mud, trees, dead wood, and leaves which the river brings down at its annual floods, which begin in the month of March, by the melting of the fnow and ice in the northern parts. This innundation continues three months. The muddy lands pro-duce long grafs, canes, and reeds in great abundance : at the over-flowings of the river, the grafs, canes, and reeds ftop great quanti-ties of the mud and rubbifh that defcend with the current. The long grafs, &c. neareft the river, muft receive a greater quantity of this rubbifh than that which is more diftant, and this caufes the bank of the Miffifippi to be higher than the interior land, and ac-counts for the waters never returning to the river; and we may rea-fonably fuppofe, that the lakes on each fide are parts of the fea, not yet filled up. Thus the land is annually raifed, and continually

gains

gains on the fea. The Balize, a fmall fort, erected by the French on a little ifland, was, in the year 1734, at the mouth of the river; it is now two miles up. In the year 1767, Don Antonio D'Ulloa erected fome barracks on a fmall ifland (to which he gave the name of Saint Carlos) for the convenience of pilots, and other purpofes, being near the fouth-eaft entrance of the river, and a more dry and higher fituation than any thereabouts. There was not the leaft ap-pearance of this ifland twenty years ago.

Before I quit this fubject, I muft obferve, that on digging ten or twelve feet in the lands I have above defcribed, large bodies of trees have been frequently found. The craw-fifh abound in this coun-try; they are in every part of the earth, and when the inhabitants chufe a difh of them, they fend to their gardens, where they have a fmall pond dug for that purpofe, and are fure of getting as many as they have occafion for. A difh of fhrimps is as eafily procured by hanging a fmall canvas bag with a bit of meat in it, to the bank of the river, and letting it drop a little below the furface of the wa-ter; in a few hours a fufficient quantity will have got into the bag. Shrimps are found in the Miffifippi as far as Natches, which is near one hundred and thirty leagues from the fea.

I have before mentioned, that the river-water is remarkably muddy: I have filled a half-pint tumbler with it, and have found a fe-diment of two inches of flime. It is, notwithftanding, extremely wholefome and well tafted, and very cool in the hotteft feafons of the year; and the rowers, who are then employed, drink of it when they are in the ftrongeft perfpiration, and never receive any bad ef-fects from it. The inhabitants of New Orleans ufe no other wa-ter than that of the river, which, by keeping in a jar, becomes perfectly clear.

The navigation of the Miffifippi is confined to veffels not draw-ing above feventeen feet water, there being little more in the deep-

eft

eſt channel on the bar, which is ſubject to ſhift very often; ſo that a pilot is conſtantly employed in ſounding. On every part of the bar there is nine feet water, and ſmall veſſels go over it without fear: frigates of thirty-ſix guns have often gone through the channel, after taking their guns out. When once a veſſel has croſſed the bar, the remainder of the navigation is very ſafe, keeping clear of the great trees, which float down with the current. When winds are contrary, veſſels make faſt to the trees on the banks of the river, and haul cloſe, there being ſufficient depth of water for any ſhip whatever. It is impoſſible to anchor without being expoſed to the danger of the great trees which come down with the current almoſt continually, but more eſpecially at the time of the floods, which if any of them ſhould come athwart hawſe, would moſt probably drive in the bows of the veſſel; and there is a certainty of looſing the anchors, as the bottom of the river is very ſoft mud, covered with ſunk logs, and is in general at leaſt ſixty fathoms deep, and this ſort of bottom and depth continues almoſt as far as the Natches; and all veſſels that enter the river, can go up within three miles of that poſt.

The merchandize neceſſary for the commerce to Natchitoches, Miſſoury, and in general the upper poſts on or near the Miſſiſippi, is carried by Batteaus, which are rowed by eighteen or twenty men, and contain about forty tons burthen; they are commonly three months going from New Orleans to the Illinois. They always go in convoys from New Orleans, and before they ſet out appoint an officer from amongſt themſelves to command them; or apply for a king's officer for that purpoſe; and whenever they put on ſhore to eat their meals, or encamp for the night, they have a regular guard mounted: they uſe theſe precautions for fear of any attack from the Indians. The Chicaſhaws formerly were very troubleſome to them. Two of theſe convoys, conſiſting of from

ſeven

feven to twelve Batteaus, go from New Orleans twice a year, viz. in the fpring and autumn.

In the fpring the Miffifippi is very high ; and tho' the current is fo ftrong that nothing can make head againft it in the middle of the river, they have an advantge by an eddy or counter-current, which runs in the bends, and clofe to the banks of the river, and greatly facilitates their voyage. The current, at this feafon, runs at the rate of fix or feven miles an hour : in autumn, when the waters are low, it in general does not run above two miles an hour, except in fome parts of the river, above the Arkanfas, where there are a great many iflands, fhoals, and fand-banks of fome miles circumference, which make the voyage more dangerous, longer, and lefs expeditious, than in the fpring ; and this makes it further neceffary, that boats fhould go in convoys, that they may affift each other in cafe of meeting with any of the accidents they are fo evidently expofed to. Great pieces of coal are conftantly found on the fand-banks, from whence it may be concluded, that there are coal-mines on the upper parts of the Miffifippi.

OF THE

POST and S·E T T L E M E N T S

ON THE

. M I S S I S I P P I.

TO proceed with order and facility in defcribing the pofts which are on the Miffifippi, and thofe which communi-cate with that river, I fhall begin with the Balize, and fo go on, afcending the river. The ifland of Saint Carlos, of which I have before´ fpoke, is near the entrance of the Miffifippi, and lies in twenty-nine degrees north latitude, and in eighty-nine degrees ten minutes longitude from the meridian of London : there are houfes for the refidence of an officer, twenty foldiers, a pilot, and a chap-lain. The reafon of eftablifhing this poft, is that affiftance may be given to veffels coming into the river, and to forward intelligence or difpatches to New Orleans : This is called the Balize as well as the French poft, which lies two miles eaft of the entrance of the river, and was originally built with the fame defign, and as a defence for the mouth of the river : its fituation (which is very low and fwampy) would never admit of any ftrong fortification ; butwhat there was, is now gone to ruin : nothing remains but the foldiers bar-racks, and three or four guns *en barbette*. From this place nothing is to be feen but low marfhes, continually overflowed, till we get within a few leagues of the Detour de L'Anglois, where there are fome few plantations, moft of which are but very late eftablifh-ments, and are, as yet, but of very little confequence. At the De-tour the river forms almoft a circle ; fo that veffels cannot pafs it with the fame wind that conducted them to it, and are obliged to wait for a fhift of wind. This gave the idea to the French, of

building

building two forts at this Pafs, one on each fide of the river, to prevent the enterprifes of any enemies; for although the forts are only enclofures of ftockades and a defence againft fmall arms, the batteries on each fide, which are of ten twelve-pounders, are more than fufficient to ftop the progrefs of any veffel, as there is no poffibility of mooring nor of making a veffel faft on fhore : the impoffibility of mooring has been before accounted for by the defcription given of the bed of the river. The going on fhore is equally impoffible, as the forts are on points of land, which are bounded by the river on one fide and by fwamps on the other, fo that any attacks againft them muft prove unfuccefsful. Such is the fituation of thefe forts, which might befides receive continual reinforcements from the inhabitants in their neighbourhood, and from New Orleans, which is but feventeen miles diftant. The authors who have wrote concerning Louifiana have given many different reafons for this place being called the *Detour des Anglois*; I fhall give that which appears the moft probable.

The officers who had been fent to reconoitre the Miffifippi, and to report the propereft place to build the capital of Louifiana on, in their return to Mobile, going down the river, faw an Englifh brig made faft to the fhore, which curiofity had induced to go thus far up, and was waiting for a fair wind to proceed on further difcoveries. The plantations and the well-built houfes on each fide the river afford a very pleafing and agreeable profpect, which continues till we arrive at New Orleans; and this, with a tolerable fair wind, is an affair of about four hours.

NEW

NEW ORLEANS.

NEW ORLEANS ſtands on the eaſt ſide of the river, and in 30°. north latitude; its ſituation is extremely well choſen, as it has a very eaſy communication with the northern parts of Louiſiana (now Weſt Florida) by means of the Bayouk of St. John, a little creek, which is navigable for ſmall veſſels drawing leſs than ſix feet water, ſix miles up from the lake Ponchartain, where there is a landing-place, at which the veſſels load and unload; and this is about two miles from the city. The entrance of the Bayouk of St. John is defended by a battery of ſix guns and a ſerjeant's guard. The veſſels which come up the Miſſiſippi haul cloſe along-ſide the bank next to New Orleans, to which they make faſt, and take in or diſcharge their cargoes with the ſame facility as from a wharf. The town is ſecured from the inundations of the river by a raiſed bank, generally called the Levée; and this extends from the *Detour des Anglois*, to the upper ſettlement of the Germans, which is a diſtance of more than fifty miles, and a good coach-road all the way. The Levée before the town is repaired at the public expence, and each inhabitant keeps that part in repair which is oppoſite to his own plantation. Having deſcribed the ſituation of the city of New Orleans, I will proceed to its plan of conſtruction.

The parade is a large ſquare, in the middle of that part of the town which fronts the river; in the back part of the ſquare is the church dedicated to St. Louis, a very poor building, framed with wood; it is in ſo ruinous a condition that divine ſervice has not been performed in it ſince the year 1766, one of the king's ſtore-houſes being at preſent uſed for that purpoſe. The capuchins are the curates of New Orleans; on the left hand ſide of the church

I   they

they had a very handfome and commodious brick houfe, which is totally deferted and gone to ruin; they now live on their planta- tion, and in a hired houfe in town.   On the right hand fide of the church is the prifon and guard-houfe, which are very ftrong and good buildings.   The two fides of the fquare were formerly occu- pied by barracks for the troops, which are entirely deftroyed.   The fquare is open to the river, and on that fide are twenty-one pieces of ordnance, en barbette, which are fired on public rejoicings. All the ftreets are perfectly ftraight, and crofs each other at right angles, and thefe divide the town into fixty-fix fquares, eleven in length by the river's fide, and fix in depth; the fides of thefe fquares are one hundred yards each, and are divided into twelve lotts, for the eftablifhment of the inhabitants.   The intendant's houfe and gardens take up the right fide of the parade, the left fide is occupied by the king's ftore-houfes and an artillery-yard.   There is at prefent no building fet on part for the governor; his general refidence is in a large houfe, which was formerly the property of the company who were the proprietors of Louifiana, known by the name of *la compagnie d'occident*.   The agent of the company is now owner of the houfe.   The convent of the Urfulines and general hofpital, which is attended by the nuns, occupy the two-left hand fquares facing the river : thefe buildings are ftrong and plain, well anfwering the purpofes for which they were defigned.   The gene- ral plan of building in the town, is with timber frames filled up with brick; and moft of the houfes are but of one floor, raifed about eight feet from the ground, with large galleries round them, and the cellars under the floors level with the ground; it is impof- fible to have any fubterraneous buildings, as they would be con- ftantly full of water.   I imagine that there are betwixt feven and eight hundred houfes in the town, moft of which have gardens. The fquares at the back and fides of the town are moftly laid out in gardens; the orange-trees, with which they are planted, are not unpleafant objects, and in the fpring afford an agreeable fmell.

The

There are, exclusive of the slaves, about seven thousand inhabitants in town, of all ages and sexes. The fortifications are only an *enceinte* of stockades, with a *banquette* within and a very trifling ditch without; these can answer no end but against Indians, or negroes, in case of an insurrection, and keep the slaves of the town and country from having any communication in the night. There are about four hundred soldiers kept for the police of the town and country; these belong to the detached companies of the marines: there are also ten companies of militia, four chosen from the inhabitants of the town, the planters and their servants form the remainder.

The government of Louisiana is composed of a governor, an intendant, and a royal council. The governor is invested with a great deal of power, which, however, on the side of the crown is checked by the intendant, who has the care of the king's rights, and whatever relates to the revenue; and on the side of the people it is checked by the royal council, whose office it partly is to see that the people are not oppressed by the one nor defrauded by the other. The royal council, who stile themselves *Le Conseil superieur de la Louisiane*, consist of the intendant, who is first judge, the king's attorney, six of the principal inhabitants, and the register of the province; and they judge in all criminal and civil matters. Every man has a right to plead his own cause before them, either verbally or by a written petition; and the evidences called on by each party attend the examination of the council. In a court like this, eloquence or great abilities cannot support injustice or confound truth.

The intendant is commissary of the marine and judge of the admiralty; and he decides, in a summary manner, all disputes between merchants, or whatever else has a relation to trade. A final reference may be made from any judgment given by the intendant

or

References.

1. *Church* . . . .
2. *Prison & Guard house* . . . .
3. *Intendants house.* . . . .
4. *House of La Compagnie*
   d'occident . . . .
5. *Governors* . . . .
6. *Powder Mag.* . . . .
7. *Arsenal for Boats.* . . . .
8. *Capuchines* . . . .
9. *Kings Store houses.* . . . . . .
10. *Ursulines.* . . . .
11. *Gen.l Hospital* . . . .
12. *Guard houses.* . . . .
The Dotted Squares are lotts not
   yet granted . . . .

Road to Germain

6

7

R I V E

600 f.t to an Inch.

There are, exclufive of the flaves, about feven thoufand inhabitants in town, of all ages and fexes. The fortifications are only an *enceinte* of ftockades, with a *banquette* within and a very trifling ditch without; thefe can anfwer no end but againft Indians, or negroes, in cafe of an infurrection, and keep the flaves of the town and country from having any communication in the night. There are about four hundred foldiers kept for the police of the town and country; thefe belong to the detached companies of the marines : there are alfo ten companies of militia, four chofen from the inhabitants of the town, the planters and their fervants form the remainder.

The government of Louifiana is compofed of a governor, an intendant, and a royal council. The governor is invefted with a great deal of power, which, however, on the fide of the crown is checked by the intendant; who has the care of the king's rights, and whatever relates to the revenue; and on the fide of the people it is checked by the royal council, whofe office it partly is to fee that the people are not oppreffed by the one nor defrauded by the other. The royal council, who ftile themfelves *Le Confeil fuperieur de la Louifiane;* confift of the intendant, who is firft judge, the king's attorney, fix of the principal inhabitants, and the regifter of the province; and they judge in all criminal and civil matters. Every man has a right to plead his own caufe before them, either verbally or by a written petition; and the evidences called on by each party attend the examination of the council. In a court like this, eloquence or great abilities cannot fupport injuftice or confound truth.

The intendant is commiffary of the marine and judge of the admiralty; and he decides, in a fummary manner, all difputes between merchants, or whatever elfe has a relation to trade. A final reference may be made from any judgment given by the intendant

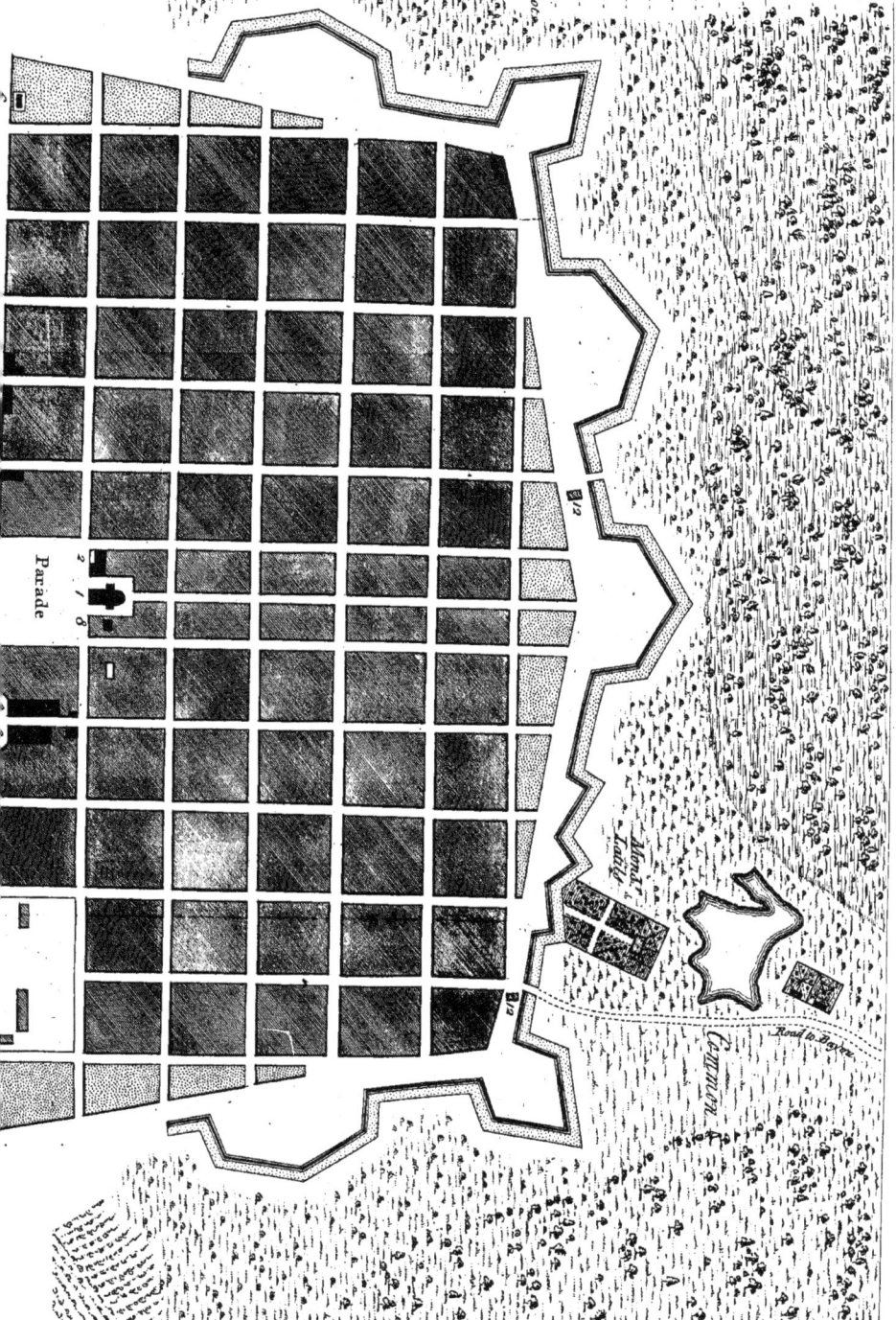

PLATE

or council to the parliament of Paris. On the firſt eſtabliſhment of the colony, nothing that could tend to render it flouriſhing or happy was unthought of. I ſhall mention one inſtance of the lenity and wiſdom of the legiſlature ; but the diſhoneſty of governors and intendants, as well as the corruption and relaxation of the govern- ment in France ſince that time, has totally perverted or ſunk into oblivion regulations that were ſo evidently calculated for the hap- pineſs of the ſubjeĉt. The planter is conſidered as a Frenchman venturing his life, enduring a ſpecies of baniſhment, and under- going great hardſhips for the benefit of his country ; for which reaſon he has great indulgence ſhewn. Whenever by hurricanes, earthquakes, or bad ſeaſons, the planters ſuffer, a ſtop is put to the rigor of exaĉting creditors. The few taxes which are levied are remitted, and even advances are made to repair their loſſes and ſet them forward. On the other hand, there can be no tempta- tion to the planter to run fraudulently into debt, to the prejudice of the French merchant, as all debts, though con- traĉted by the planters in France, are levied with great eaſe. The proceſs, properly authenticated, is tranſmitted to America, and admitted as proof there, and levied on the planter's eſtate, of what- ever kind it may be. However, care is taken that whilſt compul- ſory methods are uſed to make the planter do juſtice, the ſtate ſhall not loſe the induſtry of a uſeful member of the community ; the debt is always levied according to the ſubſtance of the debtor. Thus one party is not ſacrificed to the other, they both ſubſiſt ; the creditor is ſatisfied, and the debtor not ruined.

The paper money which circulated in this province has al- moſt effeĉted its ruin, owing to the mal-adminiſtration of Monſ, Kerlerec, who was governor during the laſt war. As the ſend- ing money from France, at that time, to pay the civil and mi- litary officers, troops, and other exigences of government, would have been attended with too much riſque, the governor and intendant were ordered to iſſue out paper money, which were

called

called Bons *, being notes for fmall fums, payable in bills of exchange, drawn at three months fight on the treafury of France.
Thefe Bons were from ten fols to one hundred livres; and whoever
collected a certain fum, as three or four hundred livres at leaft,
was entitled to a bill of exchange in lieu of the Bons, which he
paid to the treafurer of the province. The governor and intendant
empowered the commandants and commiffaries at our ports to iffue
out notes of the fame kind, for provifions, public works, and Indian prefents. Thus the debts contracted with the merchants and
inhabitants during the war amounted to very large fums, and the
abufes made of this great truft rendered the expences of the colony enormous. Monf. de Kerlerec, and fome other officers, took
opportunities of negotiating bills by way of Jamaica and other
Englifh colonies, before the peace was concluded: the amount of
thefe bills was very confiderable and was duly paid. The demands
of money from Louifiana and expences of Canada fo far ex-
ceeded all expectation, and the treafury of France being drained,
the king, by an edict in 1759, ftopped payment of this colony's
bills, to the amount of feven millions of livres, on pretence of no
authenticated vouchers, or accounts of the publick expences being
arrived. In the latter end of the year 1763, Monf. Kerlerec was
recalled, and Monf. de Rochemaure, the intendant, left the colony fome time before, and died fhortly after his arrival in France.
Monf. D'Abbadie was fent out as director-general, and was invefted with the powers of both governor and intendant: he was
inftructed to reform the abufes which had taken place in the publick offices, and to endeavour to reftore tranquility to the inhabitants, who were almoft engaged in a civil war, by entering into
the difputes of their governor and intendant, which were firft oc-

---

* The tenor of thefe Bons was as follows:

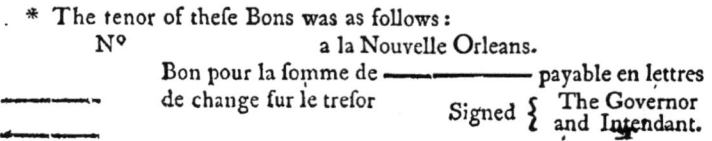

No   a la Nouvelle Orleans.

Bon pour la fomme de ———————— payable en lettres
de change fur le trefor   Signed { The Governor
                                        { and Intendant.

cafioned

cafioned by the arrival of two Englifh flags of truce, during the war, loaded with dry goods, one of which was from Jamaica and the other from Rhode Ifland. Whilft Monf. de Kerlerec held a congrefs with the Creek and Chactaw Indians at Mobile, Monf. de Rochemaure feized the veffels, imprifoned the captains and crew, and lodged the cargoes in the king's ftore-houfes. Monf. de Kerlerec on his return to New Orleans, ordered the captains and failors to be releafed, reftored their veffels to them, and permitted them to fell the cargoes for the benefit of the owners. Many of the moft refpectable inhabitants and fome officers remonftrated againft this proceeding, and reprefented the danger of admitting Englifh fubjects to trade in the time of war, who would become acquainted with the navigation of the river, and be enabled to give a true account of the then weak fituation of the province, which would fall an eafy prey to their enemies. The friends of Monf. Kerlerec, on the other hand, petitioned that the cargoes might be publickly fold, and the Englifh protected; that the colony was in the greateft want of the goods brought by the flags of truce; that it was an act of humanity in the Englifh governors who had granted thofe commiffions; that this was the only method by which they could be fupplied with what they were in the greateft neceffity for; and fhould he take harfh meafures with thefe people, the colony muft be totally excluded from all hopes of future affiftance till a peace, of which there was not then the leaft profpect. But to return to the paper money: Monf. D'Abbadie called in a great quantity of the bills of exchange and Bons, depreciating their value feventy-five per cent. and iffued out new paper money, figned by him, which he put on a par with fpecie; as, for example, a Bon of five livres was equal to one dollar or piece of eight, and feventy livres of the old paper was only equal to one dollar. Thus the induftrious planter was defrauded of three-fourths of his property.

Monf.

Monf. D'Abbadie died in February 1765, fince which the paper money iffued by him has fallen twenty-five per cent. from its original value. On the death of Monf. D'Abbadie, Monf. Aubry, commandant of the troops, fucceeded him as governor, and Monf. Foucault, *commiffaire ordonnateur*, as intendant. Thefe gentlemen continued to act in their refpective ftations, notwithftanding the ceffion of the colony to the crown of Spain in 1764. Don Antonio D'Ulloa arrived at New Orleans about the middle of the year 1766, but refufed to take the government of the colony on him, until he fhould have a fufficient armed force to eftablifh his authority. In the beginning of the year 1767 two hundred Spanifh foldiers were fent from the Havanna, but thefe he did not think fufficient to enforce his commands in a country where the Spanifh government was held in the utmoft abhorrence and deteftation ; he fent about fixty of thefe troops to erect two forts, one oppofite fort Bute, on the mouth of the Ibbeville, and the other on the weft fide of the Miffifippi, oppofite the Natches ; the remainder were fent in the autumn of 1767 to build a fort at the mouth of the river Miffoury; but the commandant was forbid to interfere with the civil government of their fettlements in the Illinois country, where Monf. De Saint Ange continues to command with about twenty French foldiers. Don Antonio D'Ulloa, who had already carried a high hand over the inhabitants, received fome orders from his court, by which the commerce of the colony was greatly reftricted, and which were fo difagreeable to the colonifts, that they revolted from the dominion of the crown of Spain ; and the council, by an edict, inferted at the end of this work, obliged him and the principal Spanifh officers to leave the province in November 1768, notwithftanding M. Aubry's remonftrances and the proteft he made againft the edict of the council.

Monf. de Sacier, one of the council, with two other gentlemen of the colony, was fent to France with this edict, and to implore

the

the protection of the king; they were imprifoned on their arrival, and have never been heard of fince.

During fix months, which elapfed before news could be received from Europe, the unhappy colonifts vainly flattered themfelves with hopes of being juftified for the fteps they had taken by the court of France. On the 23d of July, 1769, news was brought to New Orleans of the arrival of general O'Reily at the Balize, with eighteen tranfports, followed by ten more from the Havanna, having four thoufand five hundred troops on board, and loaded with ftores and ammunition. This intelligence threw the town into the greateft confternation and perplexity, as, but a few days before, letters had arrived from Europe fignifying that the colony was reftored to France.

In the general diftraction that took place, the inhabitants of the town and the adjacent plantations determined to oppofe the landing of the Spaniards, and fent couriers requiring the Germans and Accadian neutrals to join them. On the 24th an exprefs arrived from general O'Reily, which was read by Monf. Aubry to the people in church; by this they were informed that he was fent by his catholic majefty to take poffeffion of the colony, but not to diftrefs the inhabitants; and that when he fhould be in poffeffion he would publifh the remaining part of the orders he had in charge from the king his mafter; and fhould any attempt be made to oppofe his landing, he was refolved not to depart until he could put his majefty's commands in execution.

- The people, diffatisfied with this ambiguous meffage, came to a refolution of fending three deputies to Mr. O'Reily, viz. Meffrs. Grandmaifon, town-major, La Friniere, attorney-general, and De Mazant, formerly captain in the colony's troops and a man of very confiderable property; thefe gentlemen acquainted him, that the inhabitants had come to a refolution of abandoning the province,

D   and

and demanded no other favour than that he would grant them two years to remove themselves and effects. The general received the deputies with great politeness, but did not enter into the merits of their embassy, farther than assuring them that he would comply with every reasonable requeft of the colonists; that he had the interest of their country much at heart, and nothing on his part should be wanting to promote it; that all past transactions should be buried in oblivion, and all who had offended should be forgiven: to this he added every thing that he imagined could flatter the expectations of the people. On the 1st of August the deputies returned, and made publick the kind reception the general had given them, and the fair promises he had made. The minds of the people were now greatly tranquilized, and those who had before determined suddenly to quit their plantations now resolved to remain until their crops were off the ground.

During the absence of the deputies, several of the principal inhabitants applied to captain-lieutenant Campbell, late of the thirty-fourth regiment, then at New Orleans, to acquaint the governor of West Florida that they were desirous of becoming British subjects, and to beg that he would send a proper person to tender them the oath of allegiance, and to distribute the lands, on the banks of the river betwixt the Ibbeville and Natches, for them to settle on; and that they were to be joined by near two-thirds of the French inhabitants, and by German and Accadian families, of which six hundred men were capable of bearing arms. These would have proved a valuable acquisition to the province of West Florida, and it is rather unfortunate that at this time there were no troops in the forts of Natches and Ibbeville to give them protection.

On the 16th of August general O'Reily arrived at New Orleans with one frigate and twenty-two transports, and came on shore the day following to reconnoitre the ground for disembarking, and

the

the grand parade for drawing up his troops; he was attended by Monf. Aubry and the ftaff of the garrifon; he returned on board foon after, and was faluted by the frigate and the garrifon. Orders were given for the troops to difembark on the 18th, at four o'clock in the morning, by firing one gun from the frigate; ftages being previoufly made to reach from the fhore to the fides of the fhips for the foldiers to pafs over.

On a fignal being given all the troops began to move, and in lefs than ten minutes were formed on the bank of the river, and from thence marched to the grand parade, where they formed the fquare. The fhips were dreffed with the colours of different nations, and the fhrouds and yards crouded with failors. On the general's going on fhore he was faluted by the frigate, and received four cheers from the failors; and on his coming on the parade there was a general difcharge of cannon and fmall arms from the garrifon and militia, attended with mufick and drums. Don Alex. O'Reily and Monf. Aubry, with their attendants, followed by a croud of inhabitants, went to that angle of the parade where the flag-ftaff ftood. Monf. Aubry, as governor, opened his orders from his moft chriftian majefty, to deliver up the town and ifland of New Orleans, and province of Louifiana, to Don Alex. O'Reily, in the name of his catholick majefty; and expreffed his happinefs and fatisfaction in being fucceeded in the command of that country by a man of his humanity and worth; to which general O'Reily anfwered, " I fhall make it the rule of my future conduct in government, to imitate thofe wife and prudent maxims in adminiftring juftice by which you have gained the hearts of the people, even at the moft critical juncture." The Spanifh colours were now hoifted, and honoured by another general difcharge of artillery and fmall arms from the garrifon; his excellency and attendants went to church, and fung Te Deum, whilft the guards were relieving: after church was over, the parade was difmiffed, and the foldiers went to the barracks appointed for them.

On

On the 19th of Auguſt the town militia was reviewed : from this day the time was paſſed in receiving and making viſits until the 25th in the morning, when the inhabitants went to pay their reſpeĉts to their new governor ; as they entered the hall, he deſired them to place themſelves ſingly round the room, and holding a paper in his hand, containing the names of the perſons principally concerned in the late inſurreĉtion, ſuch as were preſent he begged to walk into the next room, where an officer and guard attended to take them into cuſtody ; ſuch as were abſent he ſent for, to the number of thirteen, and confined them in ſeparate apartments, ſome on board ſhip, others to guards and common priſons, where they were detained to take their trials for high treaſon ; their ſlaves and other effeĉts were ſeized in the king's name. On the 27th a proclamation was publiſhed, ordering the inhabitants to take the oaths of allegiance; and an amneſty to all concerned in the late revolt, except thoſe already in cuſtody ; and another was publiſhed prohibiting negroes from monopolizing proviſions coming to market, or buying or ſelling without a written leave from their maſters. Shortly after, other orders were given out, by which all the Engliſh ſubjeĉts, proteſtants, and Jews of every nation, were enjoined to depart from the province of Louiſiana, and all commerce prohibited, except with Old Spain and her iſlands, and neither of theſe having demand for the produce of Louiſiana and their returns, if any trade ſhould take place, could not be employed in the commerce of the Miſſiſippi.

General O'Reily made great profeſſions of friendſhip to the governor of Weſt Florida, and aſſured him, upon every occaſion, of his wiſhes to live in harmony with his Engliſh neighbours. His words and aĉtions widely differed ; he endeavoured to tamper with the Indians ſettled on our territories, and behaved with great inhoſpitality towards all Engliſh ſubjeĉts who had occaſion to go up the river Miſſiſippi, and infringed the articles of peace, by ſending a party of ſoldiers to cut the hawſers of an Engliſh veſſel, called

the

the *Sea Flower*, that had made faft to the bank of the river above the town ; the order was obeyed, and the veffel narrowly efcaped being loft. It is impoffible for veffels to navigate upon the Miffifippi, unlefs they are permitted to make faft to the fhore, as has been explained in the foregoing part of this work ; and if Englifh vef-fels are prevented, they cannot be faid to enjoy the free naviga-tion of the river, conformable to the articles of the laft peace.

In October, great and folemn preparations were made for the trial of the prifoners charged with high treafon, who continued to undergo a cruel and rigorous imprifonment until the 31ft of this month. When they were brought before the high court of juftice, as it was called, (it was more properly a court martial, the general himfelf prefiding, and the other members being moftly Spanifh officers) all the prifoners were found guilty of the charge exhibited againft them; five were fentenced to be fhot, and feven to be con-fined for ten years to the Moro caftle at the Havanna. Thofe con-demned to death were executed the day following ; their names, Monf. Lafriniere, king's attorney; Monf. De Marquis, formerly commandant of the Swifs companies at New Orleans, and knight of the order of St. Louis ; Monf. De Noyant, captain of dragoons, fon of the late king's lieutenant of Louifiana ; Pierre Careffe and Petit, merchants. The names of thofe banifhed to the Moro, Monf. De Mazant, formerly captain in the colony troops ; Monf. Garic, regifter of the council ; Meffrs. Douffet, Millet, fen. and jun. and Poupet, merchants.

Monf. Foucault, the intendant, was fent prifoner to France. Monf. Villeroy, one of the perfons firft arrefted, had embarked with his flaves and moft valuable effects, defigning to throw himfelf under the protection of the Englifh ; but being after-wards perfuaded of the fincerity of the Spanifh general's pro-mifes, he landed with his flaves and effects, and returned to his plantation : he was fo enraged at the treachery that had been ufed

towards

towards him, and at the cruel treatment he received when in confinement, that he died raving mad. The fate of Monf. Lafrinier's daughter and only child is particularly lamentable; this young lady was married but fome months before this dreadful event to Monf. De Noyant, who was handfome in his perfon, and amiable in his difpofition.

It is impoffible to reflect on this tragedy but with horror and deteftation. When fraud or treachery are made ufe of to deftroy an enemy, or punifh the guilty, it difgraces a nation and the name of juftice.

It is remarkable, that the king of Spain, in his acceptation of Louifiana, promifes the inhabitants their original form of government, and to continue the French counfellors in his council: he alfo offers to receive all the troops employed by the king of France in that country into his fervice; but the foldiers finding that they were to receive no more pay than they had formerly been allowed, which is confiderably lefs than the pay of Spanifh troops, refufed entering into that fervice to a man.

I have entered into this long digreffion concerning the government of Louifiana, with a view of giving fome idea of its prefent political ftate. I fhall now return to an account of the fettlements.

There are fome plantations on the Bayouk of St. John, and on the road from thence to New Orleans. The fettlements of Gentilly are one mile from the Bayouk of St. John, on the fide of a fmall creek, which alfo communicates with the lake Ponchartrain. Cannes, Brulé, Chapitoula, and the German fettlements join each other, and are a continuation of well cultivated plantations of near forty miles from New Orleans, on each fide of the river. At the German fettlements, on the weft fide of the river, is a church

ferved

ſerved by the capuchins ; and a ſmall ſtockaded fort in the center of the ſettlements on the eaſt ſide of the river ; an officer and twelve ſoldiers are kept there for the police of that quarter. This poſt was originally erected as an aſylum for the inhabitants who firſt ſettled there, and were much moleſted by the Chactaws and Chickaſhaws, who in alliance carried on a war againſt the ſettlers on the Miſſiſippi. Their entry into this part of the colony was very eaſy, as they went up a ſmall creek, called Tigahoe, in canoes. The entrance of this creek, which is in the lake Ponchartrain, is defended by a ſmall redoubt and a ſerjeant's guard.

Having now gone through the richeſt and moſt cultivated plantations on the Miſſiſippi, it is neceſſary to ſay ſomething of their produce, which form the greateſt part of the commerce of Louiſiana. The different articles are indigo, cotton, rice, maiz, beans, myrtle wax-candles, and lumber. The indigo of this country is much eſteemed for its beautiful colour and good quality ; the colour is brighter than that which is fabricated at St. Domingo. The cotton, though of a moſt perfect white, is of a very ſhort ſtaple, and is therefore not in great requeſt. The maiz, different ſorts of beans, rice, and myrtle candles, are articles in conſtant demand at St. Domingo.

Some of the richeſt planters, ſince the year 1762, have begun the cultivation of ſugar, and have erected mills for ſqueezing the canes ; the ſugar produced in this country is of a very fine quality, and ſome of the crops have been very large ; but no dependance can be had on this, as ſome years the winters are too cold, and kill the canes in the ground.

In the autumn the planters employ their ſlaves in cutting down and ſquaring timber, for ſawing into boards and ſcantling ; the carriage of this timber is very eaſy, for thoſe who cut it at the back
of

of their plantations make a ditch, which is fupplied with water from the back fwamps, and by that means conduct their timber to the river fide without labour; others fend their flaves up to the cyprefs fwamps, of which there are a great many betwixt New Orleans and Pointe Coupée; there they make rafts of the timber they cut, and float them down to New Orleans.

Many of the planters have faw-mills, which are worked by the waters of the Miffifippi in the time of the floods, and then they are kept going night and day till the waters fall.   The quantity of lumber fent from the Miffifippi to the Weft India iflands is prodigious, and it generally goes to a good market.

About ten leagues from the fort at the German fettlements are the villages of the Houmas and Alibamons.   The former were once a confiderable nation of Indians, they are reduced now to about forty warriors : the latter are about twenty families, being part of a nation which lived near fort Touloufe, on the river Alibamons, and followed the French when they quitted that poft in the year 1762.   One league further up is the Fourché de Chetimachas, near which is the village of a tribe of Indians of that name ; they reckon about fixty warriors.   Three leagues above this is the Conceffion of Monf. Paris, a pleafant fituation and good land; large herds of cattle are now kept there, belonging to the inhabitants of Pointe Coupée.   The new fettlements of the Accadians are on both fides of the river, and reach from the Germans to within feven or eight miles of the river Ibbeville.   Thefe are the remainder of the families which were fent by general Lawrence from Nova Scotia to our fouthern provinces; where, by their induftry, they did and might have continued to live very happy, but that they could not publickly enjoy the Roman Catholic religion, to which they are greatly bigotted.   They took the earlieft opportunity, after the peace, of tranfporting themfelves to St. Domingo

mingo, where the climate difagreed with them fo much, that they in a few months loft near half their numbers ; the remainder, few only excepted, were, in the latter end of the year 1763, re-moved to New Orleans, at the expence of the king of France.. There are about three hundred families of this unfortunate people fettled in different parts of Louifiana.

RIVER IBBEVILLE.

WE now come to the river Ibbeville, the fouth boundary of Weft Florida, and of the Englifh poffeffions on the river Miffifippi. The junction of the Ibbeville with the Miffifippi is thirty-two leagues from New Orleans, fixty leagues from the Balize, and ninety leagues from Penfacola, by the way of the lakes. The poft at the mouth of the river Ibbeville, on the banks of the Miffifippi, has ever ftruck me, from its fituation, as of the greateft confequence to the commerce of Weft Florida ; for it may with reafon be fuppofed, that the inhabitants and traders who refide at Pointe Coupée, at Natchitoches, Attacappa, Arcanfas, the Illinois, and the poft of St. Vincent's on the Ouabache, would rather trade at this place than at New Orleans, if they could have as good returns for their peltry and the produce of their country ; for it makes a difference of ten days in their voyage, which is no inconfiderable faving of labour, money, and time. The goods thefe people take in return for their peltry, furs, tobacco, tallow, and bear's oil, are, fpirituous liquors, grocery, dry goods of all kinds, and all the articles neceffary for their commerce with the favages. The only difficulty that oppofes itfelf to this neceffary fettlement is the want of a navigation through the river Ibbeville ; fo that veffels might carry on a conftant intercourfe betwixt this place and Penfacola, without going up the Miffifippi, which is a tedious navigation. The better to fhew the facility of accomplifhing this, I fhall here infert a defcription of the paffage from lake Ponchartrain to the Miffifippi, and directions neceffary to be obferved in that navigation. The coaft of Weft Florida, from Penfacola to lake Ponchartrain, is fo well known that it is not neceffary to fay any thing on that head. The defcription of the river Ibbeville, &c. was a report tranfmitted with plans and draughts, in the year 1765, to his excellency general Gage.

D E-

M A S S I A C,

PART of the RIVER AMIT,
And the RIVER IBBEVILLE.

BEFORE I begin the defcription and directions, it is neceffary I fhould mention fome errors which have fubfifted in all geographical accounts hitherto given of that part of the country, which I have examined ; thefe I will endeavour to explain. The names Maffiac, Manchaque, Afcantia, Amit, and Ibbeville, have been fo confounded, that it is with difficulty a ftranger can know what part of the country to apply one or other of them to ; and thefe errors ftill fubfift with the French, fo that when this paffage is talked of even amongft themfelves they confound one another, and he who would fpeak of that part next the Miffifippi, is thought by another to have faid fomething of the communication betwixt the lakes Ponchartrain and Maurepas. In order to avoid the fame miftakes, it is proper thefe names fhould be diftinctly feparated ; the way I think they fhould be underftood is this : The paffage from lake Ponchartrain to lake Maurepas fhould be called the Maffiac, and the two channels be diftinguifhed, by one being called the S. W. and the other the N. W. The Amit fhould carry its name as far as its current runs, which is from its fource, near Natches, to where it empties itfelf into lake Maurepas, which is feventy leagues. The Ibbeville I cannot underftand to be any thing more

E 2 than

than a fmall creek, which is fupplied with water by the Miffifippi and Amit. From March to September the former generally af- fords water enough to make a navigation through ; the reft of the year its whole fupply is from the latter, and that only for fix leagues and a half up. By this rule I fhall go on with the defcription and directions, which are as follow. Off the pafs at Maffiac, next to the lake of Ponchartrain, is found three fathoms of water ; and there are not lefs fteering W. for the center of the pafs, which when entered there is four or five fathoms, keeping mid-channel : this depth of water will be carried all the way to lake Maurepas. Two miles and a half up this channel is the point of an ifland, which is formed by two channels ; the entrance of the great chan- nel, called by the French Grand Maffiac, lies N. W. and the little one, which they call Le Petit Maffiac, N. W. by N. The great channel is the beft, although the depth of water is the fame in both ; but as the fhoals do not run fo far off the points, and as the turnings are not fo great, nor fo many, the diftance is confe- quently lefs ; for thefe reafons I fhould recommend the great chan- nel for our conftant navigation. However advantageous it may appear at firft fight to have a poft on the eaft end of the ifland, it would anfwer no purpofe, as the favages go frequently into lake Maurepas from lake Ponchartrain, by the river Tanchipao ; which for canoes and fmall boats is equally as good a navigation, becaufe about three leagues up a branch of the Nitabani empties itfelf into that river, and which is the communication from Tanchipao to lake Maurepas. The opening of the lake Maurepas is about feven miles from the eaft point of the ifland ; here it is neceffary to keep near the ifland, as a fhoal bank runs off a point that lies fouth about one mile and a half from the pafs. Steering by this di- rection, there will not be found lefs than feven feet water on the bar, and never lefs than eight feet going through the lake. The mouth of the river Amit bears weft foutherly ; by keeping near the north fhore we do not leffen the water, but come at once into four fathoms ; but go as we pleafe, we cannot find lefs than five feet.

The

The mouth of this river is remarkable from being embayed, and from a number of trees which ſtand off the land in the lake and are almoſt covered with water. The land is overflowed when the waters are high, about one foot and a half, as appears by the marks on the trees, and continues ſo near a league up the river, where there is a ſpot of land which appears to be never covered : all ſuch ſpots I have ſhewn in the annexed draught. But this is an obſervation which may be made of the country throughout ; that the lands grow lower as we advance in the woods, and at three and four hundred yards back from the river we never fail meeting with bogs and ſwamps. As the land is not much overflowed at the mouth, it would be no difficult matter to make a bank for the ſecurity of a ſmall poſt there ; and if it ſhould be ever thought neceſſary, materials are ready; there being ſhells, with which lime may be made, and very fine timber, ſuch as cypreſs and elm. As I have been very careful in making the draught, and marking every little river that empties itſelf into this, I ſhall ſay nothing of them, only that unleſs this draught is followed, or a pilot taken, miſtakes may be made by going up one of them, inſtead of the river to be purſued. The nearer we approach the junction of the Amit with the Ibbeville the current becomes ſtronger. When I went up, in the month of March, I found within about three leagues of that place a current running at the rate of three miles an hour, though at the entrance at lake Maurepas it was ſcarcely perceptible. From the mouth of the Amit to the junction of the Ibbeville ſeveral trees are fallen down, which ſhould be removed, otherwiſe the navigation is continually liable to interruptions by the logs floating down, and being intercepted by them, which in a very little time would form a barricado quite acroſs, ſuch as there was when I went up, and which was cleared by ten negroes ſent down for that purpoſe, and my detachment. The depth of water from lake Maurepas to the Ibbeville is from four to nine fathoms, and the diſtance fourteen leagues : here it is neceſſary to ſtrike the maſts when the waters are high, as the branches of the trees hang very low, and

intervene

intervene fo that in fome parts they form an arbour over the river. Four leagues further up the lands are lower than in any other part of the country, the marks of the water on the trees being ten feet above the land.   At irregular diftances, as from one to three hundred yards on each fide of the river, there are high lands overgrown with canes, and this place is called Tagoulafay ; here are a number of fmall rivulets which run into the river ; one league higher is Anatamaha, which, in the Indian language, fignifies the fifh-place: it is properly called, for they abound here all the year, which accounts for the vaft number of crocodiles that are continually on the banks of this river.   Sloops and fchooners may come as far as this place when the waters are at the loweft, here never being lefs than twelve feet water ; and at this time there is an eddy from the river Amit which fets to the weftward.   From hence to the Miffifippi I think the trees fhould be cut down forty feet back from the river fide, that a road might be made for carriages when the waters are low, at which time the bed of the river is dry from the Miffifippi ; when the waters are high it will ftill be neceffary for the navigation, as veffels may be tracked up by horfes or men to the Miffifippi, in the fame manner as lighters in England.   The river is too deep for fetting conveniently with poles, and too narrow for rowing ; and the vaft ftrength of the current, at the time of the floods, without there fhould be room for the oars, would drive the batteaux into the woods, and it would be a difficult matter to find the way back to the river.   My batteau went about one mile above Anatamaha, but I could not get her any higher, although there was not lefs than four and five feet water all the way to the Miffifippi, which is more than three leagues diftance (including the turnings of the river), and when the waters are up there will be from eleven to eighteen feet water.   At two leagues to the weftward of Anatamaha the land is never covered above one foot, which, when fecured from the inundations of the river by a bank being thrown up, will be as good as any in Louifiana, and will yield every produce natural to the climate.

More

More than fix miles of the paffage of the river Ibbeville is choaked up by wood, which has been drawn in by the eddy from the Miffifippi at the annual floods. The river, for fix miles below its entrance, is not in general above fifty feet wide ; many large trees had fallen acrofs the river, which ftopped the logs that were floating down, and fo formed a barricado. In the beginning of the year 1764, captain-lieutenant Campbell, late of the thirty-fourth regiment, undertook to clear the river, and make it navigable ; and by order of major Farmer (who at that time commanded in Weft Florida) hired upwards of fifty negroes for that purpofe. In the month of October, when the bed of the river was dry, they cut the trees which had fallen acrofs into fhort logs, and cleared a path-way on the fide of the river about eight miles down, throwing the canes and all the rubbifh into it ; expecting that when the Miffifippi fhould rife it would carry all before it. In December captain Campbell reported that he had made the river perfectly navigable. The negroes had unfortunately begun to cut the logs next the Miffifippi, and had not cleared the embarraffments that were on the lower parts of the river, which, when the floods came on, intercepted fuch logs as floated down, and made the river in a worfe condition than ever. A poft was eftablifhed in the fpring following, and a detachment of thirty foldiers of the thirty-fourth regiment, with officers, and an engineer ; they built fome huts to lodge themfelves, provifions, ftores, and Indian prefents ; and they continued to work at the river, but to as little pnrpofe as the negroes had done before. In July, the thirty-fourth regiment being on their way to the Illinois, major Farmer took off the detachment, leaving the engineer, an artillery officer, and three or four artificers, (moft of whom were in a fickly ftate) and the ftores, to the mercy of the neighbouring Indians ; who, within a few days after the departure of the regiment, pillaged the poft, and the poor defencelefs people were happy to efcape with their lives to New Orleans, leaving the artillery and fuch things as the Indians

could

could not deſtroy behind them. In the month of December, 1766, governor Johnſtone ſent a detachment of the Scots fuſileers, who were lately arrived in Weſt Florida, to repoſſeſs that poſt; they built a ſmall ſtockaded fort, which continued to be garriſoned by the troops from Penſacola in the year 1768, when I left that place. I have ſince heard that the garriſons at this poſt and Natches are withdrawn.

POINTE COUPEE.

THE settlements at Pointe Coupée commence about ten leagues from the river Ibbeville; they extend twenty miles on the west side of the Missisippi; and there are some plantations back on the side of (what is generally called) *la fausse riviere*, thro' which the Missisippi passed about sixty years ago; making the shape of a crescent, and made a difference to the voyager of near eight leagues. It is said that about that time two Canadians were descending the river, but were stopped at the beginning of this crescent by the roughness of the waves, occasioned by the wind blowing very hard against the current. One of these travellers chose to amuse himself with his gun until the wind should abate: and that he might not lose his way in the woods, he determined to follow a little brook, which had been made by the inundations of the river; he had gone but a small distance, when he again found himself by the side of the river, and saw the white cliffs before him; which he knew by the course of the Missisippi to be eight leagues from the place where he left his companion; to whom he immediately returned, and acquainted him with this discovery. They agreed to endeavour to get their canoe across, as there was about a foot water in the brook, which had a little slope towards the lower part of the river; they got their canoe into the brook, and cut away the roots of trees and bushes that obstructed its passage, and the waters of the Missisippi entering seconded their endeavours, so that in a short time they effected their purpose. It is reported that in less than six years after the Missisippi passed entirely through this channel, leaving its former bed quite dry, and which is now difficult to trace, being mostly filled up, and overgrown with trees.

The

The fort, which is a quadrangle with four baftions, is built with with ftockades, and contains a very handfome houfe for the commanding officer, good barracks for the foldiers, ftore-houfes, and a prifon. The commanding officer is chofen from one of the eldeft captains of the colony; the authority of the governor is delegated to him, and the ftorekeeper is the reprefentative of the intendant. There are feldom more than twelve foldiers at this place, who are for no other purpofe than to preferve good order. The fort is fituated on the fide of the Miffifippi, about fix miles above the loweft plantation. The church is very near the fort, and is ferved by a capuchin; there are three companies of militia in this canton, chofen from the white inhabitants, who amount to about two thoufand of all ages and fexes, and about feven thoufand flaves. They cultivate tobacco and indigo, raife vaft quantities of poultry, which they fend to the market of New Orleans, and furnifh to the fhipping; they fquare a great deal of timber and make ftaves, which they fend down in rafts to New Orleans. The inhabitants cultivated maize and other provifions on the eaft fide of the river; but after the peace, when that fide of the Miffifippi was ceded to the Englifh, fuch as had houfes there, who were but few, removed to the weft fide, which remained to the French.

TONICAS

T O N I C A S.

ON the eaſt ſide of the river, and about two miles above the laſt plantation of Pointe Coupée, is the village of the Toni-cas, formerly a numerous nation of Indians; but their conſtant intercourſe with the French, and immoderate uſe of ſpirituous liquors, has reduced them to about thirty warriors. They attacked the 22d regiment, commanded by major Loftus, when on their way to take poſſeſſion of the Illinois, on the 20th of March, 1764, at the Roche de Davion; they killed five men and wounded four, that were in two canoes which went a-head of the convoy: although they fired on the other boats they did no other damage, but prevented the regiment proceeding on its enterprize. The ſoldiers did not land, as their enemies were concealed in the wood, and their numbers unknown; they occupied both ſides of the river, and the current in the middle of the ſtream run at the rate of five miles an hour: we have been very credibly informed that ſome of the French of Pointe Coupée, and their ſlaves, aſſiſted the Tonicas in this attack.

PELOUSAS.

THE small river of Peloufas is ten leagues above the settlements of Pointe Coupée, and one league below the mouth of the river Rouge; it receives its name from the natives, and its waters from a lake which lies about forty leagues S. W. of the place where it empties itself into the Miſſiſippi. Twenty-five leagues up this river is a settlement, known by the name of Peloufas and Attacappa; it is formed by about sixty families of Accadians, diſcharged soldiers, and inhabitants from fort Touloufe, on the river Alibamons, who have a few slaves. They raiſe tobacco, maize, and wheat; the latter only for their own conſumption. They have large herds of cattle, and follow the Indian commerce. They have a small church, and a capuchin miſſionary reſides with them. This ſettlement was made under the direction of Monſ. D'Abbadie, in the year 1763, and was governed by a French officer, named Pelrin, till the year 1767, when the inhabitants, who had been oppreſſed by the tyranny, which has been always exerted by officers of that nation commanding out-poſts, complained to Don Antonio D'Ulloa, and Monſ. Aubry accuſing him alſo of ſacrilege, he having forcibly taken poſſeſſion of the plate deſtined to the uſe of the altar, and uſed it at his own table, under pretence of keeping it in ſecurity. This worked his ruin more effectually than his ill treatment of the inhabitants, and he was threatened with excommunication; however he was puniſhed by undergoing ſevere penances enjoined by the prieſts, and rendered incapable, by the ſentence of a court-martial of French officers, of any employment military or civil. The government of this ſettlement was afterwards veſted in a magiſtrate to be choſen annually by the inhabitants from amongſt themſelves. One company of militia was alſo raiſed for the defence of the eſtabliſhment, and the officers receive pay from the Spaniſh government.   4.

NATCHES.

N A T C H E S.

THIRTY-four leagues from the river Rouge is the Natches, which, from its fituation and foil, is the fineft and moft fertile part of Weft Florida. The fort is about fix hundred and feventy yards from the river's fide. The road to it is very bad, on account of a fteep high ground which is at a fmall diftance from the landing-place, very difficult to afcend, and almoft impracticable for carriages; a fmall diftance from this high land is a hill, on the fummit of which ftands the fort, and the road becomes much better, afcending with a gradual flope. The trouble of going up is recompenfed by the fight of a moft delightful country of great extent, the profpect of which is beautifully varied by a number of little hills and fine meadows, feparated by fmall copfes, the trees of which are moftly walnut and oak. The country is well watered, hops grow wild, and all kinds of European fruits come to great perfection. The fences of many of the gardens made by the French ftill remain, and feveral fruit-trees, moftly figs, peaches, and wild cherries. The French always efteemed the tobacco produced here, as preferable to any cultivated in other parts of America. This country was once famous for its inhabitants, who from their great numbers, and the ftate of fociety they lived in, were confidered as the moft civilized Indians on the continent of America. They lived fome years in great friendfhip with the French, whom they permitted to fettle on their lands, and to whom they rendered every fervice in their power. Their hofpitality was repaid with ingratitude. The French debauched, and fometimes ravifhed the women, and tyrannized over the men; every day brought them fome new difgrace. They determined to get rid of their oppreffors, and on the eve of St. Andrew, 1729, they furprifed the fort, and put the whole garrifon to death; at the fame time they made

a maf.

a maſſacre of the inhabitants, in which upwards of five hundred were killed, ſome of the women and children they made priſoners; very few of either ſex eſcaped. The whole colony armed to revenge their ſlaughtered countrymen, and they had ſeveral ſkirmiſhes with the Natches, in which the ſucceſs was various. In 1730 Monſ. De Perrier de Salvert, brother to the governor, arrived from France, with the rank of lieutenant-general in Louiſiana, and five hundred regular troops, who joined the troops and militia of the colony. This army, amounting to fifteen hundred men, went, under the command of the two brothers, to attack the nation of Natches; who, with their chiefs, determined to defend themſelves in a fort they had built near a lake which communicates with the Bayouk Dargent, lying weſt of the Natches, and north of the river Rouge. They inveſted this fort, and the Indians made a very reſolute and vigorous ſally on them, but were repulſed, after a conſiderable loſs on both ſides. The French, having brought two or three mortars, threw ſome ſhells into the fort; which making a havock amongſt their women and children, ſo terrified the Indians, unuſed to this ſort of war, that they ſurrendered at diſcretion, and were conducted to New Orleans, except a few who had eſcaped to the Chickaſhaws, with their hunters, who were providing proviſions for their garriſon. Some of the unfortunate priſoners were burnt at New Orleans, and the reſt were ſent as ſlaves to the Weſt India iſlands; ſome of whom, ſhewing their reſentment by upbraiding the authors of their miſery, were thrown into the ſea. Nothing now remains of this nation but their name, by which their country continues to be called.

When I made the ſurvey of fort Roſalia, which was in the month of Auguſt, I obſerved that the Miſſiſippi had fallen thirty-ſix feet. The breadth of the river at this place is exactly eighteen hundred and ſeventy feet, and the fort ſtands one hundred and eighty feet above the ſurface of the water. It is an irregular pentagon, without baſtions, and is built of plank of five inches thick; the buildings within the fort are a ſtore-houſe, a houſe for the officers, a barrack

for

for the foldiers, and a guard-houfe. Thefe buildings are made of framed timber, filled up with mud and barbe Efpagnole, (a kind of mofs, which grows in great abundance on all the trees in Loui-fiana) and in this country that manner of building houfes is very common. The barbe Efpagnole (which much refembles a black curly beard) is alfo made ufe of for ftuffing mattreffes.

The ditch is partly made, and partly natural ; the bottom is in moft places nineteen feet from the top of the rampart, and in many twelve and thirteen from the top of the counterfcarp ; on the north fide of the fort there is no ditch at all, but it is fenced with pickets, to prevent an enemy getting under the cover of the coun-terfcarp or into the ditch. The rampart is nearly the fame height above the pickets as it is in other parts above the bottom of the ditch. The fort received the name of Rofalia in honour to Mad. la ducheffe de Ponchartrain, whofe hufband was minifter of France when it was built.

POST of ARCANSAS.

THE fort is fituated three leagues up the river Arcanfas, and is built with ftockades, in a quadrangular form; the fides of the exterior polygon are about one hundred and eighty feet, and one three pounder is mounted in the flanks and faces of each baftion. The buildings within the fort are, a barrack with three rooms for the foldiers, commanding officer's houfe, a powder magazine, and a magazine for provifion, and an apartment for the commiffary, all which are in a ruinous condition. The fort ftands about two hundred yards from the water-fide, and is garrifoned by a captain, a lieutenant, and thirty French foldiers, including ferjeants and corporals. There are eight houfes without the fort, occupied by as many families, who have cleared the land about nine hundred yards in depth; but on account of the fandinefs of the foil, and the lownefs of the fituation, which makes it fubject to be overflowed, they do not raife their neceffary provifions. Thefe people fubfift moftly by hunting, and every feafon fend to New Orleans great quantities of bear's oil, tallow, falted buffaloe meat, and a few fkins. The Arcanfas or Quapas Indians live three leagues above the fort, on the fide of the river; they are divided into three villages; over each of which prefides a chief, and a great chief over all; they amount in all to about fix hundred warriors; they are reckoned amongft the braveft of the fouthern Indians; they hunt little more than for their common fubfiftence, and are generally at war with the nations to the weftward of them, as far as the river Bravo, and they bring in very frequently young prifoners and horfes from the Cadodaquias, Paneife, Podoquias, &c. of which they difpofe to the beft advantage.

The river Arcanfas is generally efteemed to be in the moft moderate climate of any part of Louifiana, and the lands fix leagues

up

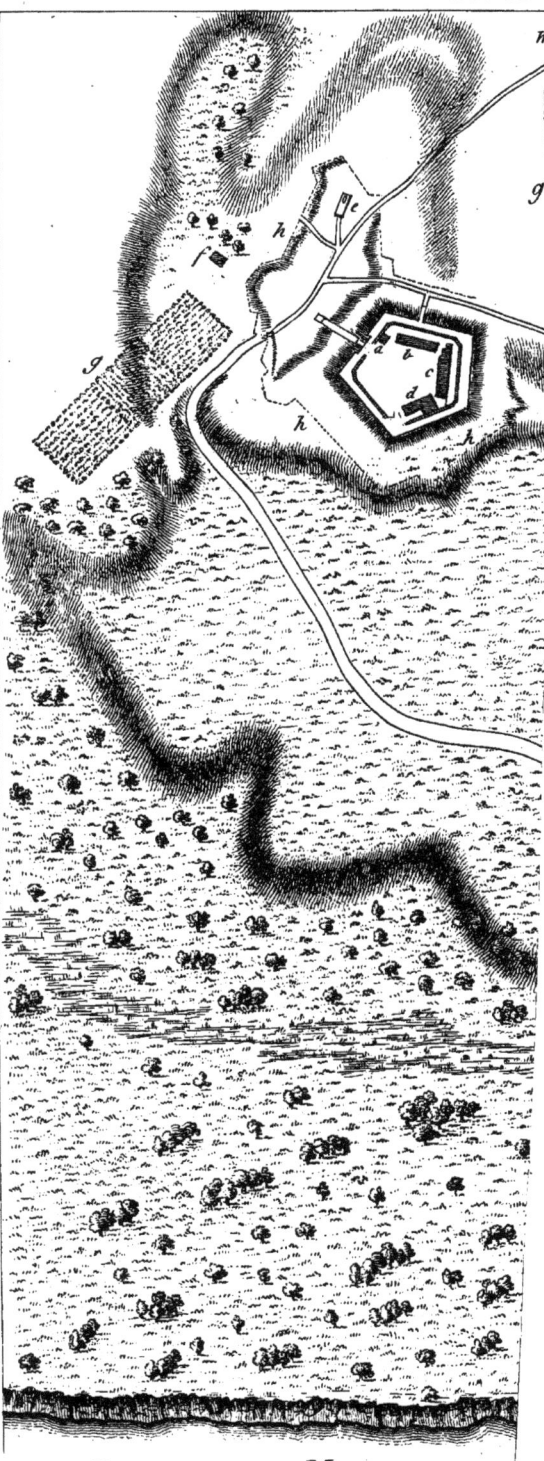

Well

g

e

h

f

g

d b c

d c

h

h

rds

and

e are

have

hich

Mary

afon

lians

adred

n In-

nce,

iem,

oung

&c.

: mo-

agues

up

RIVER MISSISI

POST of ARCANSAS.

THE fort is fituated three leagues up the river Arcanfas, and is built with ftockades, in a quadrangular form; the fides of the exterior polygon are about one hundred and eighty feet, and one three pounder is mounted in the flanks and faces of each baftion. The buildings within the fort are, a barrack with three rooms for the foldiers, commanding officer's houfe, a powder magazine, and a magazine for provifion, and an apartment for the commiffary, all which are in a ruinous condition. The fort ftands about two hundred yards from the water-fide, and is garrifoned by a captain, a lieutenant, and thirty French foldiers, including ferjeants and corporals. There are eight houfes without the fort, occupied by as many families, who have cleared the land about nine hundred yards in depth; but on account of the fandinefs of the foil, and the lownefs of the fituation, which makes it fubject to be overflowed, they do not raife their neceffary provifions. Thefe people fubfift moftly by hunting, and every feafon fend to New Orleans great quantities of bear's oil, tallow, falted buffaloe meat, and a few fkins. The Arcanfas or Quapas Indians live three leagues above the fort, on the fide of the river; they are divided into three villages; over each of which prefides a chief, and a great chief over all; they amount in all to about fix hundred warriors; they are reckoned amongft the braveft of the fouthern Indians; they hunt little more than for their common fubfiftence, and are generally at war with the nations to the weftward of them, as far as the river Bravo, and they bring in very frequently young prifoners and horfes from the Cadodaquias, Paneife, Podoquias, &c. of which they difpofe to the heft advantage.

The river Arcanfas is generally efteemed to be in the moft moderate climate of any part of Louifiana, and the lands fix leagues

up

e river Arcanſas, and
ular form; the ſides
l and eighty feet, and
faces of each baſtion.
th three rooms for the
magazine, and a ma-
commiſſary, all which
ut two hundred yards
tain, a lieutenant, and
corporals. There are
any families, who have
lepth; but on account
f the ſituation, which
t raiſe their neceſſary
ting, and every ſeaſon
r's oil, tallow, ſalted
ſas or Quapas Indians
f the river; they are
ich preſides a chief,
to about ſix hundred
t of the ſouthern In-
common ſubſiſtence,
e weſtward of them,
ery frequently young
eiſe, Podoquias, &c.

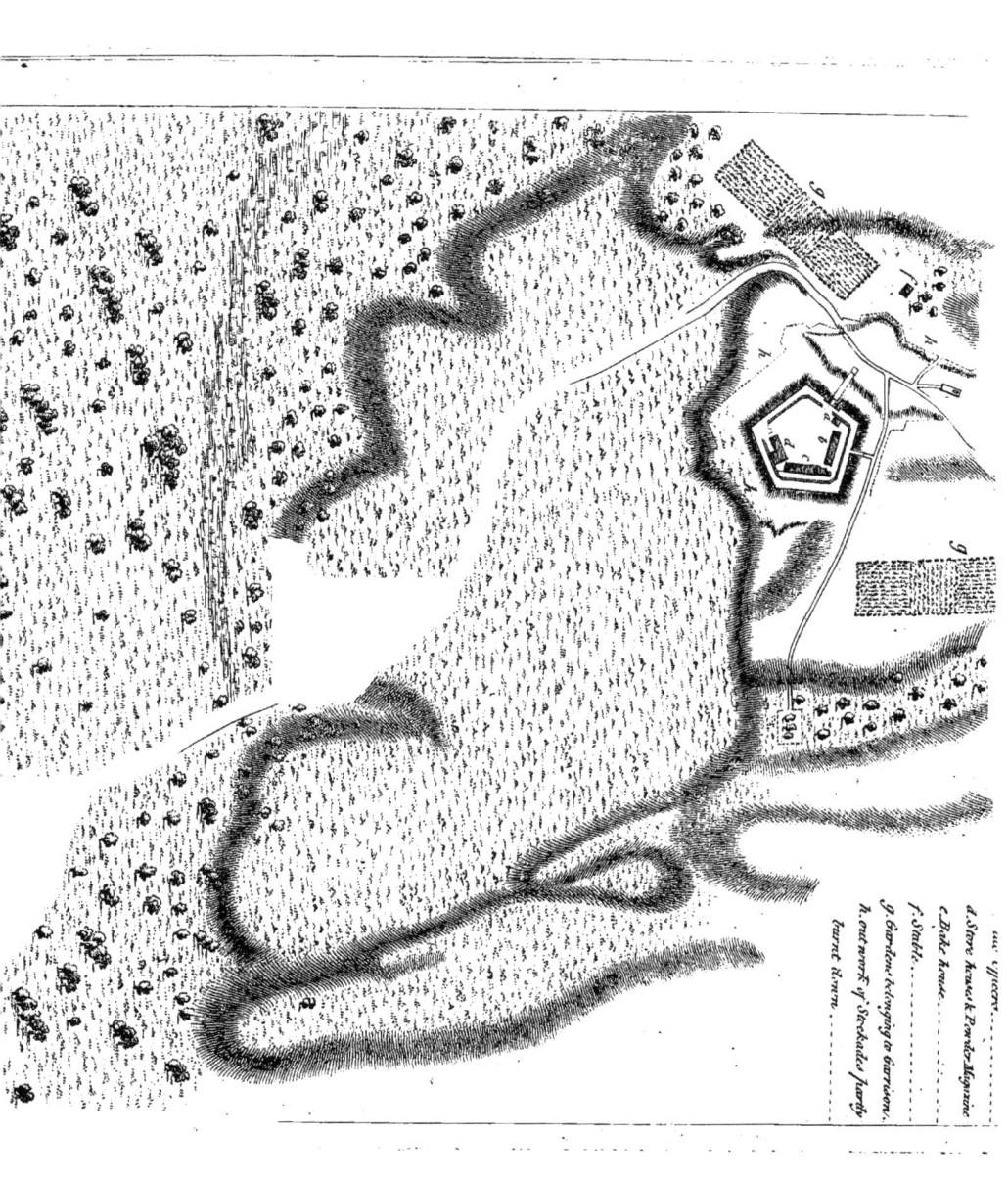

.... references ....
d. Store Arsenal & Powder-Magazine
c. Bake house
f. Stable
g. Gardens belonging to Garrison.
h. out work of Stockades partly
burnt down.

T

of th

one t

The

foldi

gazin

are ir

from

thirt)

eight

cleare

of th

make

provi

fend

buffa

live t

divide

and a

warri

dians

and a

as far

prifor

of wl

Th

derate

up the river are reckoned as fertile.   It was here that the famous Mr. Laws had his Conceffion, which was a tract of four leagues fquare; when he failed, the Germans, whom he fettled in this country, left it, being too remote.   They, on their petition, had lands granted them ten leagues above New Orleans, and which their pofterity at prefent poffefs.

There are no more fettlements or pofts near the banks of the Miffifippi, until we come to Cafcafquias, which is three hundred and feventy leagues from the fea, but generally called four hundred; it lies in the latitude 37° 43' north, and is the firft village in the country of the Illinois.

CAS-

C A S C A S Q U I A S.

THE village of Notre Dame de Cafcafquias is by far the moſt conſiderable ſettlement in the country of the Illinois, as well from its number of inhabitants, as from its advantageous ſituation ; it ſtands on the ſide of a ſmall river, which is about eighty yards acroſs ; its ſource lies north-eaſt, about ſixty leagues from the village, and fifteen leagues eaſt of the remarkable rock of Peo-rya *, and it empties itſelf with a gentle current into the Miſſiſippi, near two leagues below the village. This river is a ſecure port for large batteaux, which can lie ſo cloſe to its bank as to load and unload without the leaſt trouble ; and at all ſeaſons of the year there is water enough for them to come up. It muſt be obſerved here, that it is extremely dangerous for batteaux or boats to remain in the Miſſiſippi, on account of the bank falling in, and the vaſt number of logs and trees which are ſent down, with a violent force, by the rapidity of the current, as alſo on account of the heavy gales of wind to which this climate is ſubject. Another great advantage that Caſcaſquias receives from its river is the faci-lity with which mills for corn and planks may be erected on it : Monſ. Paget was the firſt who introduced water-mills in this country, and he conſtructed a very fine one on the river Caſcaſquias, which was both for grinding corn and ſawing boards ; it lies about one mile from the village. The mill proved fatal to him, being killed as he was working in it, with two negroes, by a party of the Cherokees, in the year 1764. The principal buildings are, the church and jeſuits houſe, which has a ſmall chapel adjoining to it ; theſe, as well as ſome other houſes in the village, are built

---

* There is in a ſort of nich in this rock a figure that bears ſome reſemblance to a man ; the Indians who paſs by pay their adorations to it, imagining it ſomething ſu-pernatural, and that it has an influence over their fortunes.

I

of

of ftone, and, confidering this part of the world, make a very good appearance. The jefuits plantation confifted of two hundred and forty *arpens* of cultivated land, a very good ftock of cattle, and a brewery; which was fold hy the French commandant, after the country was ceded to the Englifh, for the crown, in confequence of the fuppreffion of the order. Monf. Beauvais was the purchafer, who is the richeft of the Englifh fubjects in this country; he keeps eighty flaves; he furnifhed eighty-fix thoufand weight of flour to the king's magazine, which was only a part of the harveft he reaped in one year. Sixty-five families refide in this village, befides merchants, other cafual people, and flaves. The fort, which was burnt down in October 1766, ftood on the fummit of a high rock oppofite the village, and on the other fide of the river; it was an oblongular quadrangle, of which the exterior polygon meafured two hundred and ninety by two hundred and fifty-one feet; it was built of very thick fquared timber, and dove-tailed at the angles. An officer and twenty foldiers are quartered in the village. The officer governs the inhabitants, under the direction of the commandant at fort Chartres. Here are alfo two companies of militia.

LA PRAIRE DE ROCHÉS.

LA PRAIRIE DE ROCHÉS is about feventeen miles from Cafcafquias; it is a fmall village, confifting of twelve dwelling-houfes, all which are inhabited by as many families; here is a little chapel, formerly a chapel of cafe to the church at Fort de Chartres. The inhabitants here are very induftrious, and raife a great deal of corn and every kind of ftock. This village is two miles from Fort Chartres; it takes its name from its fituation, being built under a rock that runs parallel with the river Miffifippi at a league diftance, for forty leagues up. Here is a company of militia, the captain of which regulates the police of the village.

bed-chamber, and a clofet for the ftore-keeper; the latter, of a foldier's and officer's guard-rooms, a chapel, a bed-chamber and clofet for the chaplain, and an artillery ftore-room. The lines of

2.

barracks.

FORT

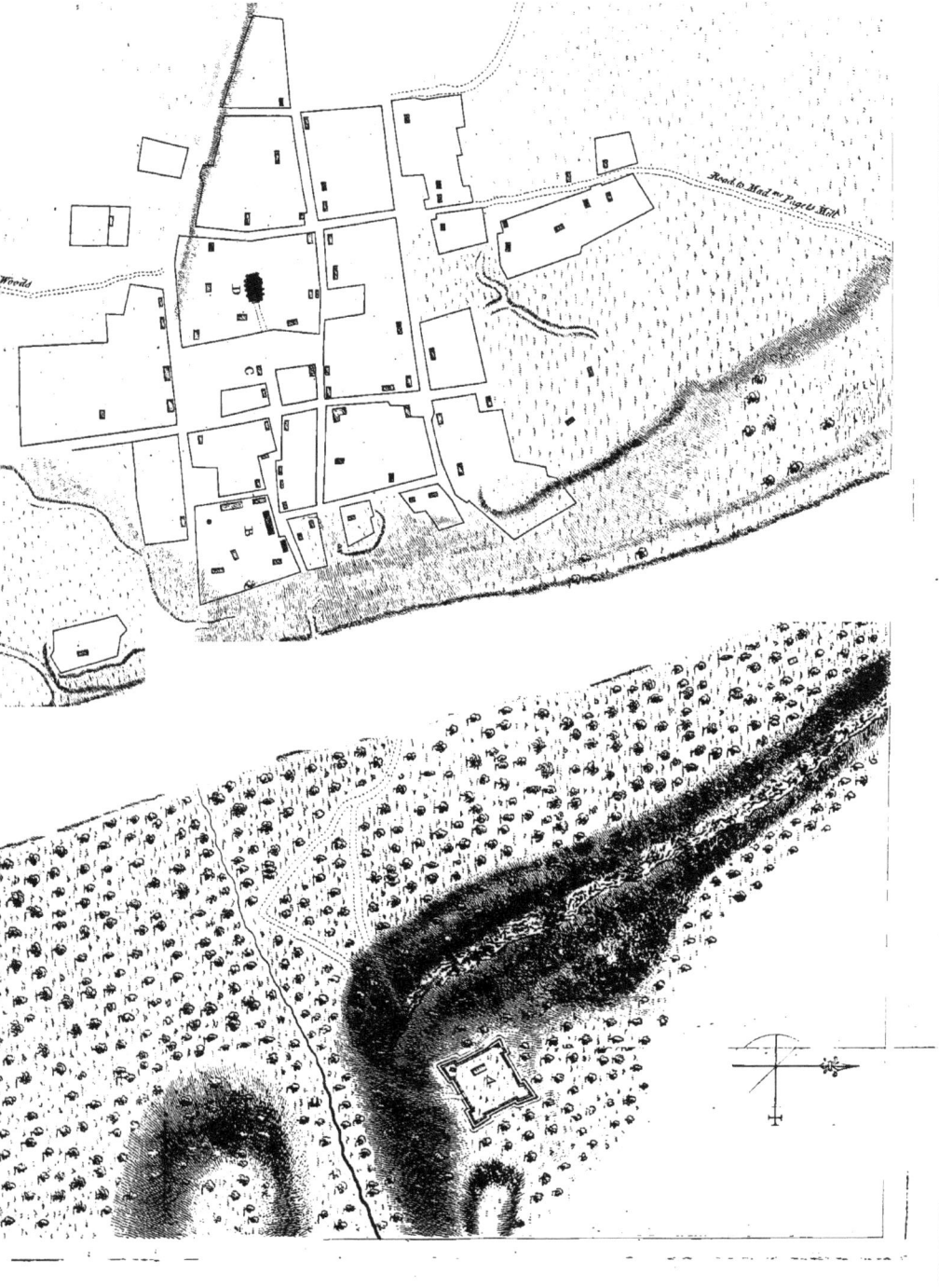

Road to Mad. mr Page's Mill

FORT

FORT CHARTRES.

FORT CHARTRES when it belonged to France was the feat of government of the Illinois; the head quarters of the Englifh commanding officer is now here, who is, in fact, the arbitrary governor of this country. The fort is an irregular quadrangle, the fides of the exterior polygon are four hundred and ninety feet; it is built of ftone and plaiftered over, and is only defigned as a defence againft the Indians, the walls being two feet two inches thick, and pierced with loop-holes at regular diftances, and with two portholes for cannon in the faces, and two in the flanks of each baftion; the ditch has never been finifhed; the entrance to the fort is through a very handfome ruftic gate : within the wall is a fmall banquette, raifed three feet, for the men to ftand on when they fire through the loop-holes. The buildings within the fort are, the commandant's and commiffary's houfes, the magazine of ftores, corps de garde, and two barracks; thefe occupy the fquare. Within the gorges of the baftions are, a powder magazine, a bakehoufe, a prifon, in the lower floor of which are four dungeons, and in the upper two rooms, and an out-houfe belonging to the commandant. The commandant's houfe is thirty-two yards long, and ten broad; it contains a kitchen, a dining-room, a bed-chamber, one fmall room, five clofets for fervants, and a cellar. The commiffary's houfe (now occupied by officers) is built in the fame line as this, its proportions and diftribution of apartments are the fame. Oppofite thefe are the ftore-houfe and guard-houfe, they are each thirty yards long and eight broad; the former confifts of two large ftore-rooms (under which is a large vaulted cellar) and a large room, a bed-chamber, and a clofet for the ftore-keeper; the latter, of a foldier's and officer's guard-rooms, a chapel, a bed-chamber and clofet for the chaplain, and an artillery ftore-room. The lines of

2.   barracks

barracks have never been finished; they at present confist of two rooms each, for officers, and three rooms for soldiers; they are good spacious rooms of twenty-two feet square, and have betwixt them a small passage. There are fine spacious lofts over each building which reach from end to end; these are made use of to lodge regimental stores, working and intrenching tools, &c. It is generally allowed that this is the most commodious and best built fort in North America. The bank of the Missisippi, next the fort, is continually falling in, being worn away by the current, which has been turned from its course by a sand-bank, now encreafed to a considerable island covered with willows: many experiments have been tried to stop this growing evil, but to no purpose. When the fort was began in the year 1756, it was a good half mile from the water-side; in the year 1766 it was but eighty paces; eight years ago the river was fordable to the island, the channel is now forty feet deep. In the year 1764 there were about forty families in the village near the fort, and a parish church, served by a Francifcan friar, dedicated to St. Anne. In the following year, when the English took poffeffion of the country, they abandoned their houses, except three or four poor families, and settled at the villages on the west side of the Missisippi, chusing to continue under the French government.

SAINT

SAINT PHILIPPE.

SAINT PHILIPPE is a fmall village about five miles from Fort Chartres, in the road to Kaoquias; there are about fixteen houfes and a fmall church ftanding; all the inhabitants, except the captain of militia, deferted it in 1765, and went to the French fide : the captain of militia has about twenty flaves, a good flock of cattle, and a water-mill for corn and planks. Tnis village ftands in a very fine meadow, about one mile from the Miffifippi.

K A O Q U I A S.

THE village of Sainte Famille de Kaoquias is generally reckoned fifteen leagues from Fort Chartres, and fix leagues below the mouth of the river Miffoury; it ftands near the fide of the Miffifippi, and is mafked from the river by an ifland of two leagues long; the village is oppofite the center of this ifland; it is long and ftraggling, being three quarters of a mile from one end to the other; it contains forty-five dwelling-houfes, and a church near its center. The fituation is not well chofen, as in the floods it is generally overflowed two or three feet. This was the firft fettlement on the river Miffifippi. The land was purchafed of the favages by a few Canadians, fome of whom married women of the Kaoquias nation, and others brought wives from Canada, and then refided there, leaving their children to fucceed them. The inhabitants of this place depend more on hunting, and their Indian trade, than on agriculture, as they fcarcely raife corn enough for their own confumption: they have a great deal of poultry and good ftocks of horned cattle. The miffion of St. Sulpice had a very fine plantation here, and an excellent houfe built on it; they fold this eftate, and a very good mill for corn and planks, to a Frenchman who chofe to remain under the Englifh government. They alfo difpofed of thirty negroes and a good ftock of cattle to different people in the country, and returned to France in the year 1764. What is called the fort is a fmall houfe ftanding in the center of the village; it differs in nothing from the other houfes except in being one of the pooreft; it was formerly enclofed with high pallifades, but thefe were torn down and burnt. Indeed a fort at this place could be of but little ufe.

DRAUGHT of the
R. Ibbeville

Being a short communication
from the SEA to the first of the
English Settlements on the

MISSISSIPPI

K A O Q U I A S.

THE village of Sainte Famille de Kaoquias is generally reckoned fifteen leagues from Fort Chartres, and six leagues below the mouth of the river Missoury; it stands near the side of the Missisippi, and is masked from the river by an island of two leagues long; the village is opposite the center of this island; it is long and straggling, being three quarters of a mile from one end to the other; it contains forty-five dwelling-houses, and a church near its center. The situation is not well chosen, as in the floods it is generally overflowed two or three feet. This was the first settlement on the river Missisippi. The land was purchased of the savages by a few Canadians, some of whom married women of the Kaoquias nation, and others brought wives from Canada, and then resided there, leaving their children to succeed them. The inhabitants of this place depend more on hunting, and their Indian trade, than on agriculture, as they scarcely raise corn enough for their own consumption: they have a great deal of poultry and good stocks of horned cattle. The mission of St. Sulpice had a very fine plantation here, and an excellent house built on it; they sold this estate, and a very good mill for corn and planks, to a Frenchman who chose to remain under the English government. They also disposed of thirty negroes and a good stock of cattle to different people in the country, and returned to France in the year 1764. What is called the fort is a small house standing in the center of the village; it differs in nothing from the other houses except in being one of the poorest; it was formerly enclosed with high pallisades, but these were torn down and burnt. Indeed a fort at this place could be of but little use.

Mississippi R.

Riv. free across

Ibbeville R.

Indian Encampment some canoes
come up as far as this.

Thus far Navigable
all the Year

2   Batteau lay here

3   Anatanaha

Tagoulasay

3

4

4

4

Riv. Amit

4

5

55 feet across

5

5

5

6

6   Ockettaholli

Axiefoea   6

70 feet across

DRAUGHT OF THE
R . Ibbeville
Being a short communication
from the SEA to the first of the
English Settlements on the
MISSISIPPI
Scale french League to 1 Inch.

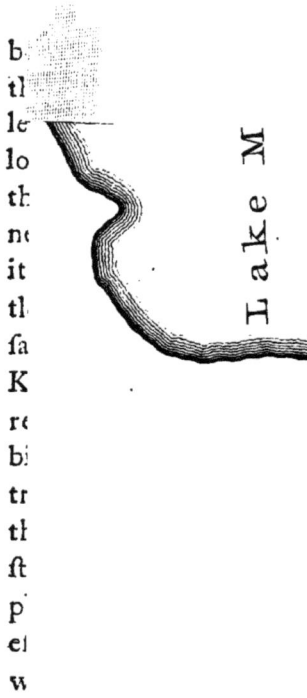

SAINT LOUIS, or PAINCOURT.

THIS village is one league and a half above Kaoquias, on the weft fide of the Miffifippi, being the prefent head quarters of the French in thefe parts. It was firft eftablifhed in the year 1764, by a company of merchants, to whom Mouf. D'Abbadie had given an exclufive grant for the commerce with the Indian nations on the river Miffoury; and for the fecurity and encouragement of this fettlement, the ftaff of French officers and the commiffary were ordered to remove there, upon the rendering Fort Chartres to the Englifh; and great encouragement was given to the inhabitants to remove with them, moft of whom did. The company has built a large houfe, and ftores here, and there are about forty private houfes, and as many families. No fort or barracks are yet built. The French garrifon confifts of a captain-commandant, two lieutenants, a fort-major, one ferjeant, one corporal, and twenty men.

SAINTE GENEVIEUVE, or MISERE.

THE firſt ſettlers of this village removed about twenty-eight years ago from Caſcaſquias : the goodneſs of the ſoil and the plentiful harveſts they reaped made them perfectly ſatisfied with the place they had choſen. The ſituation of the village is very convenient, being within one league of the ſalt ſpring, which is for the general uſe of the French ſubjects, and ſeveral perſons be- longing to this village have works here, and make great quantities of ſalt for the ſupply of the Indians, hunters, and the other ſettlements. A lead mine, which ſupplies the whole country with ſhot, is about fifteen leagues diſtance. The communication of this village with Caſcaſquias is very ſhort and eaſy, it being only to croſs the Miſſi- ſippi, which is about three quarters of a mile broad at this place, and then there is a portage, two miles diſtance, to Caſcaſquias. This cuts off eighteen miles by water, ſix down the river Caſcaſ- quias and twelve up the Miſſiſippi. The village of St. Louis is ſup- plied with flour and other proviſions from hence. An officer ap- pointed by the French commandant has the entire regulation of the police. Here is a company of militia, commanded by a Monſ. Valet, who reſides at this place, and is the richeſt in- habitant of the country of the Illinois ; he raiſes great quanti- ties of corn and proviſions of every kind ; he has one hundred ne- groes, beſides hired white people, conſtantly employed. The vil- lage is about one mile in length and contains about ſeventy families. Here is a very fine water-mill, for corn and planks, belonging to Monſ. Valet.

OF

OF THE

COUNTRY OF THE ILLINOIS.

THE country of the Illinois is bounded by the Miſſiſippi on the weſt, by the river Illinois on the north, by the rivers Ouabache and Miamis on the eaſt, and the Ohio on the ſouth.

The air in general is pure, and the ſky ſerene, except in the month of March and the latter end of September, when there are heavy rains and hard gales of wind. The months of May, June, July, and Auguſt, are exceſſive hot, and ſubject to ſudden and violent ſtorms; January and February are extremely cold; the other months of the year are moderate. The principal Indian nations in this country are, the Caſcaſquias, Kaoquias, Mitchigamias, and Peoryas; theſe four tribes are generally called the Illinois Indians: except in the hunting ſeaſons, they reſide near the Engliſh ſettlements in this country, where they have built their huts. They are a poor, debauched, and daſtardly people. They count about three hundred and fifty warriors. The Peanquichas, Maſcoutins, Miamis, Kickapous, and Pyatonons, though not very numerous, are a brave and warlike people. The ſoil of this country in general is very rich and luxuriant; it produces all ſorts of European grains, hops, hemp, flax, cotton, and tobacco, and European fruits come to great perfection. The inhabitants make wine of the wild grapes, which is very inebriating, and is, in colour and taſte, very like the red wine of *Provence*. The country abounds with buffalo, deer, and wild-fowl, particularly ducks, geeſe, ſwans, turkies, and pheaſants. The rivers and lakes afford plenty of fiſh.

H 2

In

In the late wars, New Orleans and the lower parts of Louisiana were supplied with flour, beer, wines, hams, and other
provisions from this country: at present its commerce is mostly
confined to the peltry and furs, which are got in traffic from the
Indians; for which are received in return such European commodities as are necessary to carry on that commerce and the support of the inhabitants.   2

OF THE

GOVERNMENT

OF THE

COUNTRY OF ILLINOIS,

WHEN BELONGING TO THE FRENCH.

THIS country, when in poffeffion of the French, was governed by a military officer, called the major-commandant,
who was appointed by the governor of New Orleans; he was always a man connected with the governor by intereft or relationfhip;
he was abfolute in his authority, except in matters of life and
death; capital offences were tried by the council at New Orleans:
the whole Indian trade was fo much in the power of the commandant, that nobody was permitted to be concerned in it, but on
condition of giving him part of the profits. Whenever he made
prefents to the Indians, in the name of his king, he received peltry and furs in return; as the prefents he gave were to be confidered
as marks of his favour and love for them, fo the returns they made
were to be regarded as proofs of their attachment to him. Speeches
accompanied by prefents were called *paroles de valeur*; any Indians
who came to a French poft were fubfifted at the expence of the
king during their ftay; and the fwelling this account was no inconfiderable emolument.

As every bufinefs the commandant had with the Indians was
attended with certain profit, it is not furprifing that he fpared no
pains to gain their affections; and he made it equally the intereft
of the officers under him to pleafe them, by permitting them to
trade

trade, and making them his agents in the Indian countries. If any perſon brought goods within the limits of his juriſdiction, without his particular licence, he would oblige them to ſell their merchandiſe, at a very moderate profit, to the commiſſary, on the king's account, calling it an emergency of government, and employ the ſame goods in his own private commerce: it may eaſily be ſuppoſed, from what has been before ſaid, that a complaint to the governor of New Orleans would meet with very little redreſs. It may be aſked, if the inhabitants were not offended at this monopoly of trade and arbitrary proceedings? The commandant could beſtow many favours on them, ſuch as giving contracts for furniſhing proviſions, or performing publick works; by employing them in his trade, or by making their children cadets, who were allowed pay and proviſions, and could when they were grown up recommend them for commiſſions. They were happy if by the moſt ſervile and ſubmiſſive behaviour they could gain his confidence and favour. Every perſon capable of bearing arms was enrolled in the militia, and a captain of militia and officers were appointed to each pariſh; the captain of militia regulated corvées and other perſonal ſervice. From this military form of government the authority of the commandant was almoſt univerſal. The commiſſary was a mere cypher, and rather kept for form than for any real uſe; he was always a perſon of low dependence, and never dared counteract the will of the commandant.

Grand Gouffre

Petit Gouffre

Cypriere de Couillart

Natches

Thos. Kitchin Sculpsit.

Attention Scanner:
Foldout in Book!

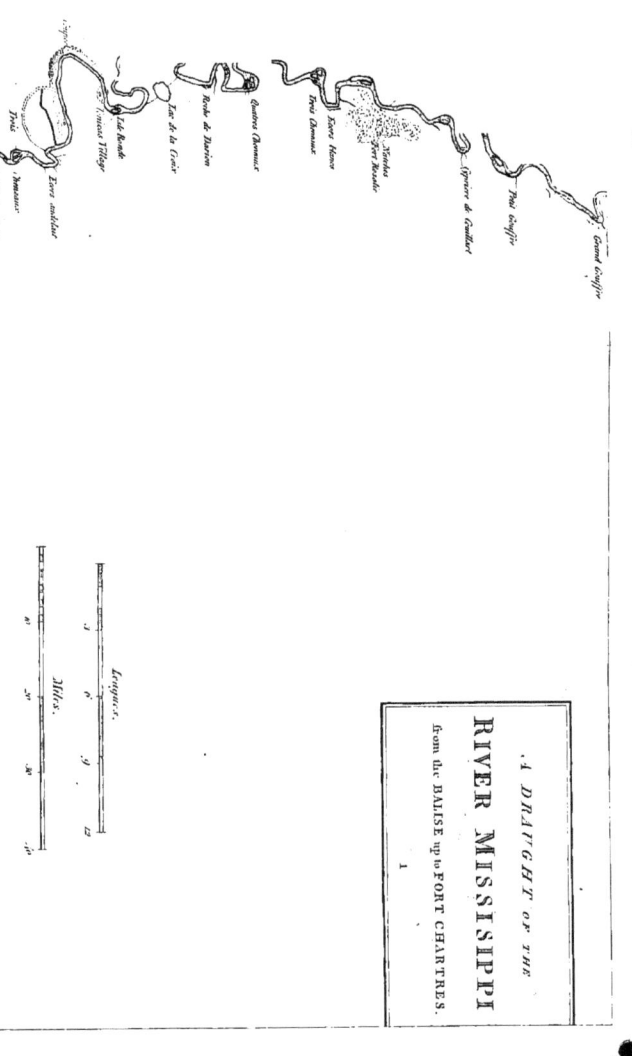

A DRAIGHT OF THE

RIVER MISSISIPPI

from the BALISE up to FORT CHARTRES.

1

Leagues.

Miles.

RES

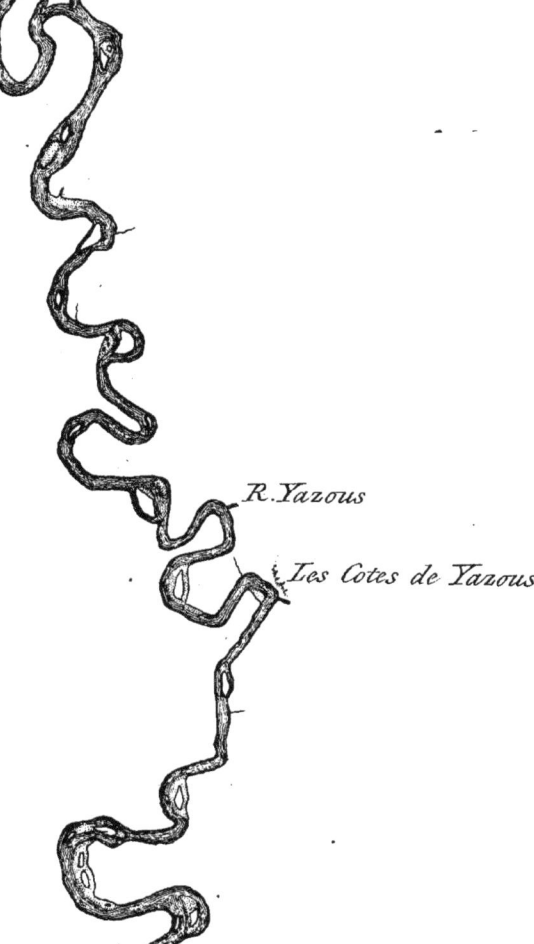

R.Yazous

Les Cotes de Yazous

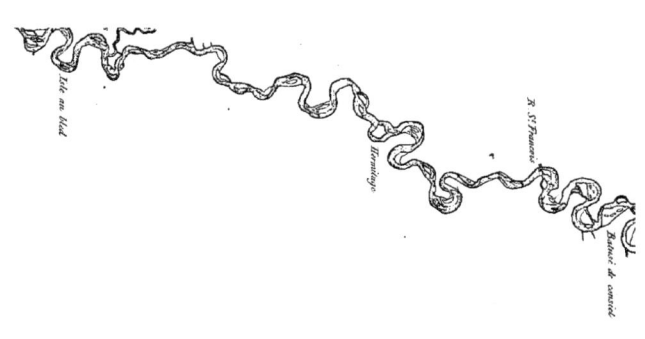

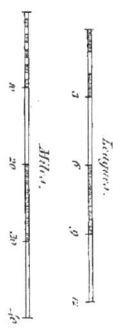

Village Savage

Fort Chartres

Grand Prairie

Vill.
lle
a

PI

St. Genevieuve

ΓRES.

on Scanner:
t in Book!

Village Sauvage
Fort Chartres

R Cascaquie

Spr. Sauvage
Kaoas
incorporés
R. aux Kaoasquoias
R. Marie

Cap. auprès Kaoas
S.t Cosme

Le Tour

Cap. à la Gauche

Cap. Girard

Anconte
frois

R. Ohio

. A DRAUGHT OF THE

RIVER MISSISIPPI

from the BALISE up to FORT CHARTRES.

3

PLAN

of

BILE

Reference.

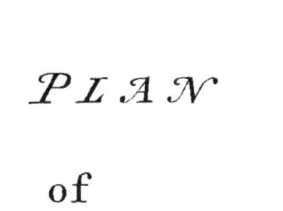

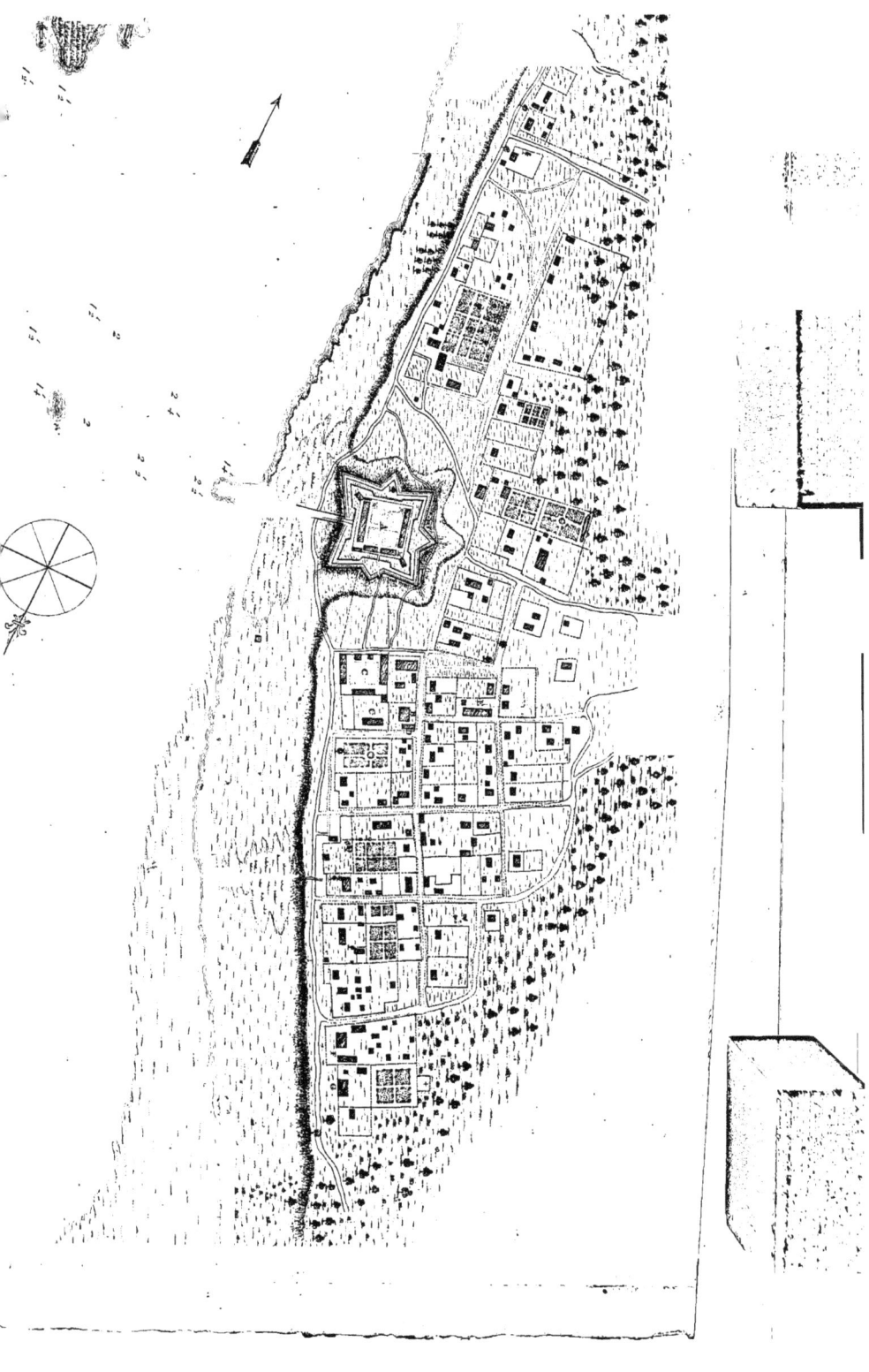

Of the INHABITANTS.

THE firſt white inhabitants of the Illinois came from Canada; ſome brought wives and families with them, others married Indian women in thoſe countries; there is ſtill a continual intercourſe between them and the Canadians. The men of theſe countries are very ſuperſtitious and ignorant; they are in general active and well made; they are as good hunters, can bear as much fatigue, and are as well acquainted with the woods, as the Indians; moſt of them have ſome knowledge of the dialeds of the neighbouring Indians and much affed their manners. The price of labour in general is very high, as moſt of the young men rather chuſe to hunt and trade amongſt the Indians, than apply to agriculture or become handicrafts. At the Illinois a man may be boarded and lodged the year round on condition of his working two months, one month in ploughing the land and ſowing the corn, and one month in the harveſt. The only trades they have amongſt them are carpenters, ſmiths, maſons, taylors, and millwrights. The number of white inhabitants in this country, excluſive of the troops, are about two thouſand, of all ages and ſexes; in this number are included thoſe who live at Fort St. Vincent's, on the Ouabache. Thirty French ſoldiers were withdrawn from thence in the latter end of the year 1764. The inhabitants at this poſt live much at their eaſe, having every thing neceſſary for their ſubſiſtence of their own produdion. Their commerce is the ſame as that of the other inhabitants of this country.

A R-

L'ARRET

DE LA

COUR SUPERIEURE DE LA PROVINCE,

Mentioné à la page 16.

LOUIS, par la grace de Dieu, roi de France & de Navarre, à tous ceux qui ces préfentes verront, fàlut : Savoir faifons, que vû par le confeil fupérieur de la province de Louifianne, les très-humbles reprefentations faites cejourd'hui à la cour, par tous les habitans, négocians, artizans, & autres peuples, icelles expofitives, que le foulagement d'un peuple dont le confeil eft le pere, le maintien des loix dont il eft le depofitaire & l'interprette, les progrès de l'agriculture & du commerce dont il eft le proteĉteur, font les motifs des reprefentations des dits habitans & negocians, &c. Quels objets pour le confeil ! Pourroit-il, après les avoir envifagez en regarder d'autres, qu'autant qu'ils concourent à favorifer ceux-là ? Qu'il fufpende pour quelques momens fes penibles travaux, pour fe livrer aux fujets qui font reprefentés aujourd'hui, comme les plus dignes de fon attention & de fon miniftere : & toï dont le profpérité fait l'objet de nos plus ardens defirs, toi qui es pour nous ce que Sparthe, Athenes, & Rome etoient pour leurs zélés citoyens; O chere patrie ! Permets nous d'acquitter une dette legitime en te confacrant ce foible tribut de notre amour ; nos cœurs vont le diĉter, une main docile va fe preter à leurs infpirations.

Sept millions de papiers royaux formoient tout le numéraire de cette colonie & la fortune des citoyens ; la privation totale de ce capital, dont S. M. fufpendit le payement par un arrêt du mois
d'Oĉtobre

A R R E T

OF THE

SUPERIOR COUNCIL of the PROVINCE,

Referred to in page 16.

LOUIS, by the grace of God, king of France and of Navarre, to all thofe who fhall fee thefe prefents, greeting, We make it known that the fuperior council of the province of Louifiana, having taken into confideration the humble reprefentations made this day to that court by all the inhabitants, merchants, artifans, and others ; and thefe laying before it, that the relief of a people, to whom the council is a father ; the fupport of the laws, of which it is the depofitory and interpreter ; and the improvement of agriculture and commerce, of which it is the patron, are the motives of the reprefentations of faid inhabitants and merchants, &c. What important objects are thefe for the council ! Can it, after having duly confidered them, give attention to any other, farther than as they contribute to favour thefe ? Let it for a few moments fufpend its labours to attach itfelf to thofe fubjects, which are now reprefented as moft worthy of its attention and its miniftry : and you, whofe profperity is the object of our moft ardent wifhes ; you who are to us what Sparta, Athens, and Rome were to their zealous citizens, O dear country ! fuffer us to pay a lawful debt, by confecrating to you this weak tribute of our love, a tribute dictated by our hearts, which are feconded by an obedient hand, ready to perform what they infpire.

Seven millions of royal paper made all the currency of this colony, and the fortune of its citizens ; the total privation of this capital, the payment of which his majefty fufpended by an edict of

the

d'Octobre 1759, a mis la province de la Louifiane dans la plus deplorable fituation. On n'entreprendra pas de faire un detail des calamités, des renverfemens des fortunes, de la ruine des familles qui
ont été les fuites funeftes de cette cataftrophe ; la cour en a fous les
yeux un tableau plus frappint qu'on ne fçauroit le peindre, toutes
les fois qu'elle s'affemble pour être les arbitres des malheureufes
victimes de cet evénement. Revenus de l'abattement dans lequel
ils avoient été plongés, les citoyens de la Louifiane commencoient
enfin à refpirer ; ils avoient envifagé la fin de la guerre comme la
fin de leurs malheurs, & vivoient dans l'efperance que le retour de
la paix auroit été le moment deftiné pour leur foulagement. L'agriculture, (difoit l'habitant) cette richeffe la plus réelle des nations,
cette fource feconde dont coulent tous les biens dont on jouit, va
être animée & reftituera au centuple pendant la paix, les pertes
que l'on a effuyé pendant la guerre ; le commerce, fans lequel
les fruits de la terre n'ont ni prix, ni valeur, va être vivifié &
protégé (difoit le negociant) douces illufions ! Projets flateurs,
qu'êtes vous devenus ? Le cultivateur, le commerçant, tous les
états de la colonie éprouvent dans la plus profonde paix, des
revers & des calamités qu'ils n'avoient point reffenti pendant une
longue & cruelle guerre. Le premier coup dont la colonie a été
frappé eft la nouvelle de la ceffion que fa majefté en a faite à
l'Efpagne ; on ne s'étonnera point fans doute, de la profonde trif-
teffe dont cet evénement a pénétré tous les cœurs ; les François
aiment leur prince par deffus toutes chofes, & un heureux préjugé
fait pancher naturellement tous les hommes vers le gouvernement
dans lequel ils font nés ; jettons une voile fur cet evénement, la
plume tombe des mains d'un François quand il veut l'approfondir.
Ce qui occupe ferieufement aujourd'hui & qui doit auffi fixer toute
l'attention de la cour, ce font les avant-coureurs des chaines dont
une nouvelle adminiftration menace les colons de la Louifiane.
Tantôt c'eft une compagnie exclufive, qui doit au préjudice de la
nation, faire le commerce de toutes les poffeffions qui reftent aux

François

the month of October, 1759; has reduced the province of Louifiana to the moft deplorable fituation. We fhall not undertake to
enter into a detail of the calamities, of the ruined fortunes, of the
downfal of families, which were the fatal confequences of that
cataftrophe ; the court has before its eyes a more ftriking picture of
thofe than it is poffible for us to paint, every time it affembles to
take cognizance of the unhappy victims of this event. Recovered
from the dejection into which they had been plunged, the citizens
of Louifiana at laft began to take heart. They had confidered the
conclufion of the war as the end of their misfortunes, and enter-
tained hopes that the return of peace would be the moment deftined
for their relief. Agriculture, faid the inhabitants, that real wealth
of a nation, that prolific fource from whence flow all the bleffings
which we enjoy, will now be revived, and will reftore a hundred
fold during the peace, the loffes which we underwent during the
war ; commerce, without which the fruits of the earth have neither worth nor value, will be revived and encouraged, (faid the
merchant) pleafing illufions ! flattering projects ! what is now become of you ! The farmer, the dealer, all ranks and claffes in the
colony, undergo, in the moft profound peace, misfortunes and calamities which they never felt during a long and bloody war. The
firft ftroke by which the colony was afflicted, was the information
it received of the ceffion made of it by his majefty to Spain : nobody, doubtlefs, will be furprifed at the profound melancholy
which this news excited in all hearts. The French love their
monarch above all things, and a happy prejudice makes all men
naturally incline to the government under which they are born.
Let us caft a veil over this event, the pen drops from the hand of a
Frenchman when he attempts to dive into it : what at prefent
ferioufly occupies and fhould engrofs the whole attention of the
court, is the apprehenfion of that flavery with which a new adminiftration threatens the colonies of Louifiana. At one time we be-
hold an exclufive company, which, to the prejudice of the nation, is empowered to carry on all the commerce of the remain-

ing

François dans l'Amerique Septentrionale ; on voit enfuite paroître un arret, qui renferme la liberté neceffaire au commerce dans les bornes les plus étroites, & defend aux François toute liaifon avec leur propre nation, tout y refpire les prohibitions & la gêne, partout les commerçans de Louifiane trouvent des obftacles à furmonter, des difficultés à vaincre & (s'il eft permis de fe fervir de cette expreffion) des ennemies de la patrie à combattre. En Europe il s'ecoule quelquefois fix mois avant qu'un armateur parvienne à fçavoir s'il obtiendra un paffeport ; on n'eft pas mieux reçu à St. Domingue lorfqu'il eft queftion d'expeditions pour ce fleuve. Mr. le Prince Monbazon, général de l'Ifle, commence à les refufer. A la Louifiane dans le centre même de la colonie, où le génie le plus borné voit au premier coup d'oeil combien elle a befoin d'encouragement & de protection, on n'eft pas plus favorifé. Le gouvernement defendit il y a près d'un an, l'importation des négres, fous pretexte que la concurrence auroit fait tort à un négociant des colonies Angloifes qui devoit en fournir. Quelle marche effrayante & deftructive ! C'eft priver la colonie de l'aliment le plus propre à fon accroiffement ; c'eft couper les racines d'une branche de commerce qui vaut feule pour la Louifiane plus que toutes les autres réunies : accrediter des femblables fiftemes, c'eft vouloir convertir en une vafte forêt des établiffemens qui ont couté des peines & des foins à l'infini. La vigilance de la cour découvrira facilement la caufe de ces contrariétés, les efforts de fon zéle la detruiront, & fon affection pour la colonie la fauvera du naufrage. La contrainte tient tout dans la langueur & dans la faibleffe, la liberté au contraire anime tout : perfonne n'ignore aujourd'hui que l'octroi des priveléges exclufifs eft à proprement parler une efpece de vampire, qui peu à peu mine le peuple, tarit le numeraire, écrafe l'agriculture, & le commerce ; voye oppreffive, qui, pour le bonheur de l'humanité, eft depuis long-tems bannie des colonies Françoifes.

Par

ing poffeffions of the French in North America; we next fee an edict make its appearance, which confines the liberty neceffary for carrying on commerce within the narroweft bounds, and forbids the French to have any connexion with their own nation; probibitions and conftraint prevail every where; the merchants of Louifiana every where meet with obftacles to furmount, difficulties to overcome, and (if it be allowable to make ufe of fuch an expreffion) enemies of their country to combat. In Europe there fometimes paffes fix months, before a perfon who fits out a veffel knows whether he fhall obtain a paffport; we have no better fuccefs at St. Domingo when expeditions to that river are in queftion : Prince Monbazon, general of the ifland, begins to refufe them. In Louifiana, in the very center of the colony, where a perfon of the meaneft genius fees at the very firft glance how much it ftands in need of encouragement and patronage, we do not meet with more favour. The government almoft a twelvemonth ago forbid the importation of negroes, upon pretext that the competition would have hurt a merchant belonging to the Englifh colonies, who was to furnifh them. How terrible and how deftructive a bargain is this! It is depriving the colony of the food beft adapted to its nourifhment ; it is cutting up by the roots a branch of commerce, which is of more confequence to Louifiana than all the reft put together : to promote fyftems of this fort is defiring to convert into a vaft foreft eftablifhments which have coft infinite pains and trouble. The vigilance of the court will eafily difcover the caufe of thefe contrarieties ; the efforts of its zeal will deftroy it; and its affection for the colony will fave it from deftruction. Conftraint keeps the affairs of the province in a ftate of languor and weaknefs ; liberty, on the contrary animates all things : nobody is at prefent ignorant that the granting of exclufive privileges may be juftly confidered as a fort of devouring fire, which imperceptibly undermines and confumes the people, drains the currency, and crufhes agriculture and commerce ; an oppreffive method, which, for the honour of humanity, has been long fince banifhed from the French colonies.

2

To

Par quelle fatalité faut-il que la Louifiane feule voie renaître des étincelles d'un feu fi devorant. Ce ne font point içi dés terreurs paniques, la cour en demeurera convaincue après qu'elle aura pris lecture de l'arrêt dont on a l'honneur de lui prefenter l'extrait. On ne balance point à dire que l'execution du plan qu'il renferme ruineroit la colonie, en portant à l'agriculture & au commerce les plus dangereufes atteintes. Les colons de la Louifiane defpérent d'avance du falut de leur patrie, fi les privéléges & exemptions, dont elle a joui jufqu'à prefent, ne font maintenus ; fi l'exécution de ce fatal arrêt qui a porté l'allarme & la defolation dans tous les cœurs n'eft detournée ; fi une ordonnance rendue au nom de S. M. C. & publiée à la Nouvelle Orleans le 6 Septembre 1766, dont on joint ici copie, n'eft annullée comme illegale dans tous fes points, & contraire à l'accroiffement de l'agriculture & du commerce : fi enfin l'on permettoit que les douces loix fous lefquelles les colons ont vécu jufques à aujourd'hui fuffent violées. On ne doit jamais oublier le difcours fublime qu'un magiftrat illuftre addreffe aux légiflateurs de la terre (voulez-vous dit-il abroger quelque loy, n'y touchez que d'une main tremblante. Obfervez tant de folemnités, apportez tant de précautions que le peuple en conclut naturellement, que les loix font bien faintes puifqu'il faut tant de formalités pour les abroger.)

Qu'il eft douloureux fans doute pour des François, d'éprouver toutes les rigueurs aux quelles on foumet aujourd'hui leur commerce, pendant qu'une nation étrangere, leur ambitieufe rivale, fait ouvertement & fans trouble le commerce de la colonie au prejudice de la nation à qui elle appartient, qui a contribué à fon établiffement & qui en fait les fraix : on ne craint point qu'on objecte que les François feuls, ne font point en état de fournir le continent de fes befoins ; un prêt de fept millions que les citoyens de la Louifiane ont fait au roi, depuis l'année 1758, jufqu'en 1763, fera

un

To what fatality is it owing that Louifiana alone fees fparks of this devouring fire again ftruck out ? Thefe are not panick terrors, and this the court will be convinced of, after perufing the fentence, an extract of which we have here the honour of prefenting them with. We fhall not fcruple to affirm, that the carrying the plan which it contains into execution, would ruin the colony, by giving agriculture and commerce the moft dangerous wounds. The inhabitants of Louifiana defpair beforehand of the prefervation of their country, if the privileges and exemptions which it has hitherto enjoyed are not continued; if the execution of this fatal decree, which has alarmed all hearts and filled them with confternation, is not prevented; if an ordonnance publifhed in the name of his Catholic majefty at New Orleans on the 6th of September 1766, of which a copy is here fubjoined, is not annulled, as illegal in all thefe points, and an obftruction to the increafe of agriculture and commerce; if in fine the mild laws, under which the inhabitants have lived till now, were fuffered to be violated. We fhould never forget the fublime difcourfe, which a renowned magiftrate addreffes to the legiflators of the earth; "-Are you, fays he, defirous of abrogating any law, touch it with a trembling hand. Obferve fo many formalities, have recourfe to fo many enquiries, that the people may naturally conclude that the laws are facred, fince fo many precautions are required in the abrogation of them."

We will likewife, without hefitation, affirm that it is a high mortification for Frenchmen to fuffer all the rigours to which their commerce is fubjected, whilft a foreign nation, their ambitious rival, openly carries on the trade of the colony, to the prejudice of the nation to which it belongs, which contributed to its eftablifhment, and which is at the expence of it : we do not fear that it will be objected, that the French alone are not able to fupply the continent with all the commodities which they want; a loan of feven millions, which the inhabitants of Louifiana have made the king fince the year 1758 to 1763, will be an eternal monu-

4   ment

un monument éternel de l'étendue du commerce François & de l'attachment des colons pour le service de leur souverain.

Que c'est au moment qu'une nouvelle Mine vient d'être decouverte, que le cotton dont la culture assurée par l'experience, promet au cultivateur la recompense de ses travaux, & à l'armateur le chargement de ses navires, que la fabrique de l'indigo peut aller de pair avec celle de Saint Domingue, que le commerce des pelleteries est poussé au plus haut point où il soit encore parvenu, c'est dans ces heureuses circonstances que quelques ennemis de la patrie & créateurs d'un faux sisteme, ont sans doute surpris la religion des personnes en place, pour sacrifier les habitans de la Nouvelle Orleans. Que la cour ne renvoye pas à des tems plus éloignés le soulagement d'un peuple qui lui est cher ; qu'elle fasse connoître aux personnes revétues de l'autorité royale, l'épuisement ou seroit reduite cette province si elle n'étoit point desormais affranchie des prohibitions qui la plongeroit dans une ruine irremédiable ; que penseroit-on d'un médecin, qui ayant le remede universel attendroit une peste pour s'en servir. Que c'est à la faveur de la navigation des isles du vent, & sous le vent, que les habitans de la Louisiane trouvent chaque année le debit de quatre-vingt à cent cargaisons de bois ; qu'on ôte cette branche de commerce, on prive la colonie d'un revenu annuel de cinq cent mille livres au moins, somme que le travail seul des négres & l'application du maître produit sans autre mise dehors. Qu'il vaudroit mieux, suivant un fameux auteur, perdre dans un grand royaume cent mille hommes par une faute de politique, que d'en commettre une qui arrête le cours de l'agriculture & du commerce : que l'on sçait que ceux qui présentent des projets pour obtenir des priviléges exclusifs, ne manquent jamais de raisons plausibles pour les faire paroitre œconomiques & avantageux, soit au roi, soit au public ; mais l'experieuce de tous les siécles & de tous les lieux démontre evidemment

ment of the extent of the French commerce, and of the attachment of the people of the colonies to their fovereign's fervice.

It is juft at the inftant that a new mine has been difcovered, when the culture of cotton, improved by experience, promifes the planter the recompenfe of his toil, and the perfon who is concerned in fitting out veffels, cargoes to load them ; when the manufacture of indigo may vie with that of St. Dominico ; when the fur trade has been carried to the higheft degree of perfection ; it is in thefe happy circumftances that certain enemies to their country, and broachers of a falfe fyftem, have doubtlefs drawn in perfons in public office to facrifice the inhabitants of New Orleans. The court fhould not longer defer the relief of a people which is dear to it ; it fhould make known to thofe invefted with royal authority the exhaufted ftate to which this province would be reduced, if it was not for the time to come freed from the prohibitions, which would plunge it into irremediable ruin. What fhould we think of a phyfician, who being poffeffed of the panacea, or univerfal remedy, fhould wait for a plague in order to apply it ? It is by the trade to the Leeward Iflands that the inhabitants of Louifiana find means every year to difpofe of fourfcore or a hundred loads of wood ; if this branch of trade was to be taken away, the colony would be deprived of an annual income of 300,000 livres at leaft, a fum which the work of the negroes and the application of the mafter produces alone, without any foreign affiftance. According to the obfervation of a celebrated author, it would be better to lofe a hundred thoufand men in a great kingdom by an error in politicks, than to be guilty of one which fhould ftop the progrefs of agriculture and commerce. It is well known that thofe who prefent plans to obtain exclufive privileges, are never without plaufible reafons to make them appear faving and advantageous, as well to the king as the public ; but the experience of all ages and all countries evidently demonftrates, that thofe who feek exclufions,

K   have

ment que ceux qui follicitent des exclufions ont uniquement en vue leur intérêt particulier; qu'ils font moins zelés que les autres pour le bien de l'état & moins bons patriotes. Que l'execution de l'arrêt pour le commerce de la Louifiane réduiroit les habitans à l'affligeante alternative, ou de perdre leurs recoltes, faute de navires pour en faire l'exportation, ou de changer leurs denrées en fraude avec une nation étrangere, en s'expofant à fubir la rigueur de la loi qui prononce la perte des biens & de la liberté contre les contrebandiftes; quelle vie! & quel combat! Qu'il n'eft que trop vrai comme on l'a déjà obfervé, que le bruit feul de la nouvelle ordonnance a caufé une diminution confiderable, non feulement fur les objets de luxe, mais auffi fur les biens fonds. Une maifon qui valoit ci-devant vingt mille livres auroit de la peine aujourd'hui d'en produire cinq; on dira peut-être que la rareté de l'argent contribue auffi à cette diminution, mais combien fera plus grande la difette des efpéces, lorfque la colonie fe verra livrée, foit à une compagnie exclufive, foit à l'ambition de cinq à fix particuliers qui ne forment qu'une maffe? Ce fera alors un membre qui s'accroitra monftrueufement aux depens de la fubftance des autres qui deviendront fecs, & paralitiques; le corps fe verra par là menacé d'une deftruction totale : que ce n'a été qu'en favorifant ouvertement l'introduction des négres que l'on étoit parvenu à mettre cette colonie dans l'embonpoint, ou l'on l'a vue en 1759. Qu'on dira peut-être, pour diffiper les allarmes, que l'or & l'argent qui s'eft repandu fur la place, au moyen d'une nouvelle adminiftration, pourra dédommager des pertes de l'agriculture, & du commerce, mais qu'à juger de l'avenir par l'experience du paffé & du préfent, on trouvera cette reffource bien foible, perfonne n'ignorant d'ailleurs que, parmi les différens tréfors que la terre renferme dans fon fein, l'or & l'argent ne font ni les premieres richeffes, ni les plus defirables, ces matieres ont reduit dans un état déplorable leurs poffeffeurs naturels & les maîtres de ces efclaves ne font pas devenus plus puiffants. Il femble que dès le moment ils ayent perdu tout efprit d'induftrie, tout.

aptitude.

have their private intereſt ſolely in view; that they have leſs zeal than others for the proſperity of the ſtate, and have leſs of the ſpirit of patriotiſm. The execution of the decree with regard to the commerce of Louiſiana, would reduce the inhabitants to the ſad alternative of either loſing their harveſts for want of veſſels to export them, or to exchange their commodities in a fraudulent manner with a foreign nation, expoſing themſelves to undergo the rigour of the law, which ordains that thoſe who carry on a contraband trade ſhall loſe both their lives and liberties. What a life is this! what a ſtruggle! It is but too true, as has been already obſerved, that the report of the new ordinance alone has cauſed a conſiderable diminution, not only in the articles of luxury, but likewiſe in landed eſtates. A houſe which was heretofore worth twenty thouſand livres would hardly ſell for five thouſand : ſome will, perhaps, aſſert that the ſcarcity of money contributes likewiſe to this diminution; but how much greater will be the ſcarcity of ſpecie, when the colony ſhall either be delivered up to an excluſive company, or to the ambition of five or ſix individuals, who form but one body? It will reſemble a member grown to a monſtrous bulk at the expence of the ſubſtance of the reſt, which would become withered and paralytic; the body would thereby find itſelf threatened with a total deſtruction : it was only by openly favouring the introduction of negroes that this colony was raiſed to the flouriſhing ſtate which it appeared to have attained in 1759. Perhaps it will be ſaid, to diſpel theſe ʼalarms, that the gold and ſilver which has been made to abound in the place by a new adminiſtration, may indemnify for the loſſes of agriculture and commerce; but to judge of the future by the experience of the paſt and the preſent, that reſource will be found to be very weak, as nobody can be ignorant, that amongſt the various treaſures which the earth contains in its boſom, gold and ſilver are neither the chief riches nor the moſt deſirable; theſe metals have reduced their natural poſſeſſors to a deplorable ſtate, and the maſters of thoſe ſlaves are not thereby become more powerful. They appear from that moment to have loſt all ſpirit and induſtry, all diſpoſition

to

aptitude au travail, comme un laboureur qui trouveroit un tréfor au milieu de fon champ abandoneroit pour toujours la charrue ; que d'ailleurs combien d'actes de rigueur n'ont pas été éxercées contre des paifibles citoyens par un étranger, qui, quoique revétu d'un caractére refpectable, n'a fatisfait à aucuns des formalités ni à aucuns des devoirs prefcrits par l'acte de ceflion, leur objet de tranquilité. On citera un ancien capitaine qui a été detenu, par fes ordres, aux arrêts & fon navire dans le port pendant l'efpace de huit à dix mois, pour n'avoir pas fçu lire dans les decrets de la providence que le bâteau dans lequel il avoit envoyé des paquets qu'on lui avoit confié, feroit naufrage. Une femblable tyrannie a été exercée par le dépofitaire de cette même autorité informe & illegale, envers deux capitaines de la Martinique qui n'avoient commis d'autre crime, que celui de n'avoir pas deviné que le confeil de la Louifiane avoit rendu un arrêt qui interdifoit l'entrée des négres créolifés des Ifles du Vent & fous le Vent : quel traitement un ancien citoyen n'a-t-il pas effuyé à l'occafion d'un paquet qui avoit été remis au capitaine de fon navire, & qui ayant été contrarié par les vents, n'a pû le remettre à la Havanne ? Comment décrira-t-on l'inhumanité avec laquelle ont été ménés les Accadiens ? Ce peuple, le jouet des evénemens, s'eft déterminé, par un efprit patriotique, d'abandonner tout ce qu'il pouvoit poffeder fur les terres Angloifes pour venir vivre fous les heureufes loix de leur ancien maître : ils font arrivés à grand fraix dans cette colonie ; à peine font-ils parvenus à deffricher l'emplacement neceffaire à une pauvre chaumiere que, fur quelques reprefentations qu'ils ont voulu faire à M. Ulloa, il les a menacé de les chaffer de la colonie & de les faire vendre comme des efclaves pour payer les rations que le roi leur avoit donné, en enjoignant aux Allemands de leur refufer retraite. On laiffe à décider, fi cette conduite ne tient point de la barbarie ; mais on croit pouvoir conclure, fans rien exagérer, qu'elle eft diametralement oppofée au fifteme politique qui veut que l'on favorife

to work ; like a labourer who fhould find a treafure in the midft
of his field, and thereupon forfake his plough for ever. Befides,
how many acts of feverity have been exercifed againft peaceable
citizens by a ftranger ; who, though invefted with a refpectable
character, has obferved none of the formalities, nor performed any
of the duties prefcribed by the act of ceffion, their object of tranquility. We fhall mention an old captain of a fhip who was confined by his orders, and his veffel detained in the port during eight
or ten months, for not having been able to read in the decrees of
providence, that the veffel in which he had difpatched certain
packets entrufted to his care would be caft away. A fimilar tyranny was exercifed by the perfon invefted with this illegal and
unjuft authority, againft two captains belonging to Martinico, who
had been guilty of no other crime but that of not having gueffed
that the council of Louifiana had iffued an edict, which forbid the
entrance of the negroes naturalized amongft the Creolians into the
Leeward Iflands. What ill ufage has an old citizen fuffered upon
account of a pacquet, which had been put into the hands of the
captain of one of his fhips, who, having met with contrary winds,
was unable to deliver it at the Havannah ? How fhall we defcribe
the barbarity with which the people of Accadia were treated ? This
people, the fport of fortune, were determined, by a patriotic fpirit,
to forfake all they might be poffeffed of upon the Englifh territories, in order to go to live under the happy laws of their ancient
mafter : they arrived in this colony at a great expence, and fcarce
had they cleared out a place fufficient for a poor thatched hut to
ftand upon, when in confequence of fome reprefentations, which
they happened to make to Mr. Ulloa, he threatened to drive them
out of the colony, and have them fold for flaves, to pay the rations which the king had given them, at the fame time directing
the Germans to refufe them a retreat. The court is left to deter-
mine whether this conduct does not border upon barbarifm ; but
we think we may take upon us to conclude that it is diametrically
oppofite to the political fyftem, which directs us to promote every
branch

favorife toutes les branches de populationes. Ceux qui fe plaignent, & quel homme affez anéanti fous le joug peut effuyer fans murmure de telles inhumanités ? Oui, on l'ofe dire, ceux qui fe plaignent font menacés d'être emprifonnés, exilés à la Balifes, & envoyés aux mines. Que fi M. Ulloa a été revétu de quelque autorité, fon prince ne lui a jamais ordonné de la rendre tirannique, ni de l'exercer avant d'avoir fait connoître fes titres & fes pouvoirs. De telles vexations ne font pas l'ouvrage des cœurs des rois, elles s'accordent peu avec l'humanité qui fait leur caraétére & qui dirige leurs aétions : qu'on n e finiroit point fi on entreprenoit le detail de toutes les humiliations que les François de la Nouvelle Orleans ont éprouvé. Il eft à defirer, pour l'honneur de la nation, que ce qui a pû en tranfpirer puiffe être effacé par les precieux effets de la proteétion du confeil fupérieur que l'on reclame aujourd'hui, & que pour mettre le comble à tant de tribulations on leur predit, qu'avec le tems, on reduira les colons de la Louifiane à la fimple nourriture de la tortilla, tandis que l'aliment le plus fobre ne fera jamais leur peine. Que cependant le confervation de leurs jours, leurs obligations envers leurs créanciers, leur honneur émanant du patriotifme & de leur devoir, leurs fortunes enfin fe trouvant attaquées par le dit décret, les portent à offrir leurs biens & leur fang pour conferver à jamais le doux & inviolable titre de citoyen François. Que tout cet expofé les conduit naturellement à des conclufions auxquelles le zéle de la cour pour le bien public, fa fermeté pour le maintien des loix dont S. M. T. C. l'a établie depofitaire, les affure qu'elle fera l'accueil le plus favorable. Mais avant d'entrer dans ces conclufions ils doivent rendre homage aux bontés de M. Aubry. Les vœux du public fe font toujours accordés avec le choix du prince à lui donner le commandement en chef de la Louifiane, fes vertus lui ont fait décerner le titre d'honnête homme & de gouverneur equitable : il n'a jamais ufé de fes pouvoirs que pour faire le bien, &

tout

branch of population. Thofe who complain, (and who is there-
fo far broke to the yoke as to bear without murmuring fuch horrid
inhumanities ?) yes, we dare to declare it, thofe who complain are
threatened with imprifonment, banifhed to Balifes, and fent to the
mines. Now, though Mr. Ulloa might have been invefted with
fome authority, his prince never commanded him to exert it in a.
tyrannical manner, nor to exercife it before he had made known
his titles and his powers. Such oppreffions are not dictated by the
hearts of kings ; they agree but ill with that humanity which con--
ftitutes their character and directs their actions. We fhould hardly
ever make an end, were we to enter into a detail of all the mor-
tifications which the French of New Orleans have undergone. It
were to be wifhed for the honour of the nation, that as many of
them as have tranfpired might be obliterated by the precious effects-
of the protection of the fuperior court, which is now applied for,
and that to render fo much tribulation complete, it fhould be
fortold to them, that in time the inhabitants of Louifiana will be
reduced to live upon turtle alone, whilft the moft frugal fort of.
food will now be a punifhment to them. In the mean time, the
prefervation of their lives, their obligations to their creditors, their
honour, which is the refult of patriotifm and of their duty, in fine,.
their very fortune being attacked by the faid decree, reduce them
to offer their poffeffions and their blood to preferve for ever the
clear and inviolable title of Frenchmen. All that has hitherto been.
faid leads them naturally to make demands or requefts to which
the zeal for the public good, its fteddinefs in fupporting the laws
which his moft chriftian majefty has made them the depofitories of,.
affures them that it will give the moft favourable reception. But
before they proceed to thefe demands, they muft pay their homage
to the goodnefs of Monf. Aubry. The wifhes of the public have always correfponded with the choice of the prince in affigning him the
chief command over the province of Louifiana; his virtues have caufed
the titles of honeft man and equitable governor to be adjudged
him; he never made ufe of his power but to do good, and all
unjuft

tout ce qui a été injufte lui a toujours paru impoffible. Qu'ils ne craignent point qu'on ait à leur reprocher que la reconnoiffance les ait fait exagérer en quelques chofes : negliger des louanges meritées, c'eft voler une dette legitime, & concluent enfin en fuppliant le cour,

1. D'obtenir que les privéléges & exemptions dont la colonie a joui, depuis la retroceffion que la compagnie en fit à S. M. T. C. foient maintenus fans qu'aucune innovation puiffe en arrêter le cours, & troubler la fureté des citoyens.

2. Qu'il foit accordé des paffeports, congés & permiffions emanant de meffieurs le gouverneur &⁻commiffaire ⁻de S. M. T. C. aux capitaines de navires qui s'expedieront de cette colonie pour tel port de France & de l'Amerique que ce puiffe être.

3. Que tout bâtiment expédié de tel port de France & de l'Amerique que ce puiffe être, aura l'entrée libre du fleuve; foit qu'il vienne directement pour cette colonie, ou qu'il y aborde de Relâche, afin que cela s'eft toujours pratiqué.

4. Que la liberté du commerce avec toutes les nations qui font fous la domination de S. M. T. C. foit accordé à tous les citoyens, en conformité des ordres du roi à feu M. D'Abbadie, enrégiftrés au greffe de cette ville, & conformément auffi à la lettre de monfeigneur le duc de Choifeuil au même M. D'Abbadie, en datte du 9 Fevrier 1766.

5. Que M. Ulloa foit declaré infractaire & ufurpateur, en plufieurs points, de l'autorité dévolue au gouvernement & au confeil, puifque toutes les loix, ordonnances & coutumes, veulent que cette autorité ne foit exercée par aucun officier, qu'après qu'il aura rempli toutes les formalités preferites, & c'eft à quoi M.
Ulloa

unjuſt deeds have to him ever appeared impoſſible. They are not afraid of being reproached that gratitude has made them exaggerate in any particular: to neglect deſerved praiſes is to keep back a lawful debt, and they conclude, in fine, by intreating the court,

1. To obtain that the privileges and exemptions, which the colony has enjoyed ſince the ceſſion, which the company made to his moſt chriſtian majeſty, ſhould be ſupported without any innovations being ſuffered to interrupt their courſe and diſturb the ſecurity and quiet enjoyment of the citizens.

2. That paſſports and permiſſions ſhould be granted from the governors and commiſſioners of his moſt chriſtian majeſty, to ſuch captains of veſſels as ſhall ſet ſail from this colony to any ports of France or America whatever.

3. That any ſhip which ſails from any port of France or America whatever, ſhall have free entrance into the river, whether it ſail directly for the colony, or only put into it occaſionally, as has been always obſerved.

4. That the freedom of trade with the ſeveral nations under the government of his moſt chriſtian majeſty, ſhall be granted to all the citizens, in conformity to the king's orders to the late Mr. D'Abbadie, regiſtered at the ſecretary's office of this city, and likewiſe in conformity to the letter of his grace the duke de Choiſeuil, addreſſed to the ſame Mr. D'Abbadie, and dated the 9th of February 1766.

5. That Mr. Ulloa ſhall be declared to have, in many points, infringed and uſurped the authority which had devolved to the government and the council, becauſe all the laws, ordonances, and cuſtoms, direct, that the ſaid authority ſhall not be exerciſed by any officer, till he ſhall have performed all the formalities pre-

L   ſcribed,

Ulloa n'a point fatisfait ; pourquoi, il doit être declaré infractaire
& ufurpateur, 1. Pour avoir fait arborer pavillon Efpagnol en plufieurs endroits de la colonie, fans avoir préalablement montré &
fait enrégiftrer au confeil, les titres & pouvoirs dont il a pû être
munis & que les citoyens affemblés ayent pû en être informés.
2. Pour avoir, de fon chef & autorité privée, exigé que des capitaines de navires fuffent détenus & leurs batimens dans le port fans
aucun fondement & pour avoir faire mettre aux arrêts à bord d'une
fregate Efpagnole des citoyens François. 3. Pour avoir fait tenir
des confeils, dans la maifon du fieur Detrehan, par des officiers
Efpagnols, dans lefquels il a été rendu des arrêts concernant les citoyens de la Louifiane ; & demandent, qu'en vertu de tous ces
griefs & tant d'autres de notoriété publique & auffi pour la tranquilité de tous les citoyens qui reclament la protection du confeil,
ils foient affranchis deformais de la crainte d'une autorité tiranique
& des conditions portées par le dit décret, au moyen de l'éloigne-
ment de M. Ulloa, auquel il doit être enjoint de s'embarquer, dans
le premier batiment qui partira, pour fe rendre où bon lui femble-
ra, hors de la dependance de cette province.

6. Qu'il foit ordonné à tous les officiers Efpagnols, qui font dans
cette ville ou repandus dans les poftes dépendans de la colonie, d'en
fortir pour fe rendre également là ou ils jugeront à propos, hors de
la dependence de la dite province, & qu'enfin il plaife à la cour, or-
donner que l'arrêt à intervenir fera lû, publié & affiché dans tous
les lieux & endroits accoutumés de cette ville & copies collationées
envoyées dans tous les poftes de la dite colonie. Les dites repréfentations font fignées par cinq cent trente fix perfonnes, habitans,
négotians, marchands, & notables. Vû auffi la copie du décret publié par ordre de S. M. C. non fignée, ni dattée, autre copie d'une
ordonnance

fcribed ; and this condition Mr. Ulloa has not complied with. He fhould therefore be declared to have infringed and ufurped the authority of the government ; 1. For having caufed Spanifh colours to be fet up in feveral parts of the colony, without having previoufly caufed to be regiftered in the council books, the titles and powers which he might have received, and of which the affembly of the citizens might have been informed. 2. For having of his own accord, and by his own private authority, infifted upon captains of veffels being detained with their fhips in the port without any caufe, and for having ordered fubjects of France to be confined aboard a Spanifh frigate. 3. For having caufed councils to be held in the houfe of Mr. Detrehan by Spanifh officers, in which decrees were iffued concerning the inhabitants of Louifiana. And they requeft, that on account of thefe grievances, and many others publickly known, and likewife for the tranquility of all the citizens who apply for the patronage of the council, they fhall for the time to come be freed from the fear of a tyrannical authority, and exempted from obferving the conditions enjoined by the faid decree, by means of the difmiffion of Mr. Ulloa, who fhould be ordered to embark aboard the firft veffel which fhall fet fail, in order to depart, whenever he thinks proper, out of the countries depending upon this province.

6. That orders fhall be given to all the Spanifh officers who are in this city, or fcattered up and down at the pofts depending upon the colony, to quit them, in order to repair likewife, whenever they fhall think proper, out of the dependencies of the province ; and, finally, that the court would be pleafed to order that the decree fhall be read, publifhed, and fet up, in all the ufual places of this city, and collated copies fent to all the pofts of the faid colony. The faid reprefentations figned by five hundred and thirty-fix inhabitants, eminent merchants and dealers. On account, likewife, of the copy of the decree, publifhed by orders of his catholic majefty, neither figned nor dated, and of another copy of an

ordonance

ordonnance publiée en cette ville par ordre de M. Ulloa, du 6 Septembre 1766, l'arrêt interlocutoire rendu le jour d'hier fur le requifitoire de M. le procureur general du roi, portant & ordonnant avant dire droit, que les dites repréfentations feroient mifes entre les mains de meffieurs, M^ue Uchet, écuyer, fieur de Knion, & Piot Delaunay, confeillers titulaires, pour être par eux examinées & enfuite communiquées meffieurs les gens du roi, pour être requis & ordonné ce qu'il appartiendra de droit ; le tout vû, M. le procureur general du roi s'eft levé & remis, a dit,

" Meffieurs,

" Le premier point le plus intéreffant à examiner, eft la de-
" marche de tous les habitans & negocians unis, qui dans leur
" fervitude préparée, & leurs malheurs démontrés, s'addreffent à
" votre tribunal & vous demandent juftice des infractions faites à
" l'acte folemnel de ceffion de cette colonie : votre tribunal eft-il
" compétant ? Sont-ils fondés ? Je vais prouver l'étendue de l'au-
" torité royale déférée au confeil fupérieur. Les parlemens & les
" confeils fuperieurs font les dépofitaires des loix à l'abri defquels
" les peuples vivent heureux ; font protecteurs nés par état des
" vertueux citoyens, & font établis pour faire exécuter les ordon-
" nances, édits, & déclarations, des rois après leur enrégiftrement :
" telle a été la volonté de Louis le bien-aimé, notre feigneur roi,
" & au nom duquel tous vos arrêts jufqu'à ce jour, ont été rendus
" & mis à exécution. L'acte de ceffion, feul titre dont le commif-
" faire de S. M. C. puiffe fe prevaloir pour réclamer autorité &
" propriété fut addreffé à défunt M. D'Abbadie, avec ordre de le
" faire enrégiftrer au confeil fupérieur de la colonie, afin que les
" différens états de la dite colonie foient informés de fon contenu &
" qu'ils puiffent y avoir recours au befoin, la préfente n'étant à au-
" tres

ordonance publifhed in this city, by order of Mr. Ulloa, of the 6th of September 1766, the interlocutory decree iffued yefterday, upon the requifition of the king's attorney-general, orders and directs, that before the decifion of the court, the faid reprefentations fhall be put into the hands of Meffrs. Attre Uchet, efquire, lord of Knion, and Piot Delaunay, titular counfellors, to be by them examined, and afterwards communicated to the king's council; that what the law directs may be enacted concerning them. All thefe particulars being taken into confideration, the king's attorney-' general ftood up and faid,

" Gentlemen,

" The firft and moft interefting point to be examined is the ftep
" taken by all the inhabitants and merchants in concert, who,
" being threatened with flavery, and labouring under grievances
" which have been enumerated, addrefs your tribunal, and re-
" quire juftice for the violations of the folemn act of the ceffion of
" that colony. · Is your's a competent tribunal? Are thefe com-
" plaints juft? I fhall now fhew the extent of the royal authority
" vefted in the fuperior council. The parliaments and fuperior
" council are the depofitaries of the laws, under the protection of
" which the people live happily; they are, by their rank and
" dignity the patrons of virtuous citizens, and they are eftablifhed
" for the purpofe of executing the ordonances, edicts, and decla-
" rations of kings after they are regiftered. Such was the will
" and pleafure of Lewis the well-beloved, our fovereign lord, in
" whofe name all your decrees to the prefent day have been iffued
" out and carried into execution. The act of ceffion, the only
" title of which his catholic majefty's commiffary can avail him-
" felf, to make his demands *auctoritate & proprietate*, was ad-
" dreffed to the late Mr. D'Abbadie, with orders to caufe it to be
" regiftered in the fuperior council of the colony, to the end that
" the different claffes of the faid colony may be informed of its
" contents, and may be enabled to have recourfe to it upon occafion;

" this

" tres fins. La lettre de M. Ulloa dattée de la Havanne du 10
" Juillet 1765, qui caractérife fes defirs de rendre à meffieurs les
" habitans tous les fervices qu'ils pourront fouhaiter, vous fût ad-
" dreffée, meffieurs, avec priere de faire participer aux dits habitans
" qu'en cela il ne feroit que remplir fon devoir & flater fon in-
" clination. La dite lettre fût, par votre arrêt de delibéré, publiée,
" affichée, & enregiftrée comme un garant que les habitans auroient
" de leur bonheur & de leur tranquilité. Une autre lettre du mois
" d' Octobre dernier écrite à M. Aubry, conftate que la juftice fe
" rende toujours dans la colonie au nom du roi Louis le bien-aimé.
" Il réfulte du puiffant point d'appui de l'acte folemnel de ceffion
" & des autres acceffoires, que meffieurs les habitans & negocians
" font bien fondés à vous prefenter leurs très humbles repréfenta-
" tions, & vous, meffieurs, très autorifés à prononcer. Exami-
" nons actuellement avec fcrupule l'acte de ceffion, & la lettre de
" M. Ulloa ecrite au confeil fupérieur. Je crois devoir rapporter
" mot à mot l'extrait de la lettre du roi, qui fut publiée, affichée,
" & enregiftrée.

" Ce même acte folemnel de ceffion qui donne titre de propriété
" à S. M. C. ftatue pour les colons des priviléges anciens & con-
" nus, & la parole royale de notre feigneur roi, en promet & en
" fait efpérer de nouveaux dont les malheurs de la guerre l'ont privé
" de faire jouir fes fujets, les priviléges anciens étant fuprimés par l'au-
" torité du commiffaire de S. M. C. la propriété devient caduque;
" l'acte de ceffion par pure, fimple & bonne amitié s'eft fait avec fes
" referves qui confirment les priviléges & libertés, & promet aux ha-
" bitans une vie tranquile, à l'abri de leurs loix canoniques & civiles.
" La propriété refultant d'une ceffion par don gratuit, ne peut fe repéter
" & être obtenu qu'en fatisfaifant pendant toute la propriété aux referves

7   " contenues

" this inſtrument being calculated for no other purpoſe. The
" letter of Mr. Ulloa, dated from the Havannah July 10, 1765,
" which intimates his diſpoſition to do the·inhabitants all the ſer-
" vices they can defire, was addreſſed to you, gentlemen, with a
" requeſt to intimate to the ſaid inhabitants, that therein he would
" only difcharge his duty and gratify his own inclinations. The
" ſaid letter was, by your decree, publifhed, ſet up, and regiſtered,
" as a pledge to the inhabitants of happineſs and tranquility.
" Another letter, of the month of Oⱥober laſt, written to Mr. Aubry,
" certifies that juſtice ſhould be always adminiſtered in the co-
" lony in the name of Louis the well-beloved. It reſults from
" the ſolid baſis of the folemn aⱥ of ceſſion and other acceſſories,
" that the inhabitants̄and merchants have good reaſon to preſent
" you with their moſt humble remonſtrances ; and you, gentle-
" men; fully authorized to pronounce thereupon. - Let us now
" accurately examine the aⱥ of ceſſion and the letter written by
" Mr. Ulloa to the fuperior council. I think it likewife incum-
" bent on me to cite, word for word, the extraⱥ of the king's
" letter, which was publifhed, ſet up, and regiſtered.

" This very folemn aⱥ of ceſſion, which gives the title of pro-
" perty to his catholic majeſty, eſtablifhes for the inhabitants of
" the colony ancient and known privileges, and the royal word of
" our fovereign lord the king promiſes, and gives us ground to
" hope for, others, which the calamities of war have prevented
" him from making his fubjeⱥs enjoy. The antient privileges
" having been fuppreſſed by the authority of his catholic majeſty's
" commiſſioner, property becomes precarious ; the aⱥ of ceſſion,
" through pure good will and friendfhip, was made with theſe
" reſerves, which confirm their liberties and privileges, and pro-
" miſes the inhabitants a life of tranquility, under the proteⱥion
" and fhelter of their canon and civil laws. The property which
" reſults from a ceſſion by free gift cannot be claimed and ob-
" tained, except by complying with the reſerves contained in the
" ſaid

" contenues dans le dit acte de ceſſion. Notre ſeigneur roi, eſpere
" & ſe promet en conſequence de l'amitié & de l'affeĉtion de
" S. M. C. qu'elle voudra bien donner des ordres à ſon gouverneur
" & à tous autres officiers employés à ſon ſervice dans cette colonie
" pour l'avantage & la tranquilité des habitans de cette même co-
" lonie, & qu'ils ſoient jugés & leurs biens régis ſuivant les loix,
" formes & uſages de la colonie. Les titres de M. Ulloa peuvent
" ils faire prevaloir des ordonnances & des ordres infraĉtaires au
" reſpeĉt dû à l'aĉte ſolemnel de ceſſion. Les priviléges anciens,
" la tranquilité des citoyens François, les loix, formes & uſages
" de la colonie ſont ſacrés par une promeſſe royale, par un enré-
" giſtrement ordonné au conſeil ſupérieur, & par une publication
" notoire & preſcrite. Le recours à l'aĉte de ceſſion par les dif-
" férens états de la colonie, eſt l'unique fin de la lettre de notre
" ſeigneur roi ; rien de mieux fondé & de plus legal que le droit
" de repréſentations, acquis par autorité royale aux habitans &
" citoyens de la colonie.

" Paſſons à l'examen de la lettre de M. Ulloa, écrite au conſeil
" ſupérieur de la Nouvelle Orleans en datte du 10 Juillet 1765.
" Je rapporterai mot à mot l'article concernant M. le conſeil ſu-
" perieur & meſſieurs les habitans.

" *Je me flate d'avance qu'elle pourra me proportionner des occaſions*
" *favorables pour vous témoigner les deſirs qu'ils m'aſſiſtent de pouvoir*
" *vous rendre tous les ſervices, que vous & meſſieurs les habitans*
" *pourront ſouhaiter, de quoi je vous prie de les aſſurer de ma part, &*
" *qu'en cela ne ferai que remplir mes devoirs & flater mon inclination.*

" M. Ulloa a prouvé par là les ordres qu'il avoit reçu de S. M. C.
" conformes à l'aĉte ſolemnel de ceſſion, & il annonçoit un ſenti-

6   ment

" faid act of ceffion, during the time of poffeffing that property.
" Our fovereign lord the king hopes, and promifes himfelf, that
" in confequence of the friendfhip and affection fhewn by his
" catholic majefty, that he will be pleafed to give orders to his
" governor, and to all other officers employed in his fervice in that
" colony, for the advantage and tranquility of the inhabitants of
" the colony, and that they fhould be ruled and their fortunes
" and eftates managed according to the laws, forms, and cuftoms
" of the colony. Can Mr. Ulloa's titles give weight to ordinances
" and orders which violate the refpect due to the folemn act of
" ceffion? The antient privileges, the tranquility of the fubjects
" of France, the laws, forms, and cuftoms of the colony, are
" rendered facred by a royal promife, by a regiftering ordered by
" the fuperior council, and by a publication univerfally known.
" The recourfe had to the act of ceffion by the different claffes of
" the colony is the fole aim of the letter of our fovereign lord the
" king ; nothing can be better grounded or more legal than the
" right of remonftrating, which the inhabitants and citizens of
" the colony have acquired by royal authority.

" Let us proceed to an examination of the letter of Mr. Ulloa,
" written to the fuperior council of New Orleans, dated the 10th
" of July, 1765. (I fhall here cite, word for word, the article
" relative to the fuperior council and the inhabitants.)

" *I flatter myfelf beforehand, that it will be able to procure me*
" *favourable opportunities to teftify to you my defires of having it in my*
" *power to do you all the fervice that you and the inhabitants can wifh,*
" *which I beg you would affure them of from me, and let them know*
" *that in acting thus I fhall at once difcharge my duty and gratify my*
" *inclinations."*

" Mr. Ulloa proved thereby the orders which he had received
" from his catholic majefty, conformable to the folemn act of

M   " ceffion,

" ment indifpenfable à tout gouverneur qui veut bien fervir fon
" roi dans les colonies. Specialement fans habitans point de com-
" merce, fans commerce peu d'habitans. Le rapport des deux
" induftries à la maffe de l'état, étaye les trônes. La liberté & la
" concurrence font meres nourrices des deux états ; l'exclufion, le
" tiran & le maratre. Sans liberté peu de vertus. Du defpotifme
" nait la pufillanimité & l'abime des vices. L'homme n'eft re-
" connu pêcher vis-à-vis de Dieu, que parce qu'il conferve le
" libre arbitre, où eft la liberté des habitans & des négoçians ? Les
" marques de protection & de bienveillance font converties en
" defpotifme : une feule autorité veut tout anéantir. Tous les
" états fans diftinction ne doivent plus, fans courir rifque d'être
" taxés de crime, que trembler, être affervis & ramper : le confeil
" fupérieur, boulevard de la tranquilité des citoyens vertueux, ne
" s'eft foutenu que par la probité, le defintéreffement des ma-
" giftrats, & la confiance réunie des citoyens en eux. Sans prife
" de poffeffion, fans l'enrégiftrement indifpenfable au confeil fupé-
" rieur des titres & patentes fuivant les loix, formes, & ufages de
" la colonie & de la préfentation de l'acte de ceffion, M. Ulloa a
" fait juger par un prefident, trois confeillers, & un greffier, nom-
" més d'office des faits de la compétence du confeil fupérieur &
" concernant des citoyens François. Vingt fois les mecontente-
" mens, & defagremens fembloient vous forcer à vous demettre de
" vos places, mais vous avez toujours regardé annexé à votre état
" de confeiller du roi très-chretien, d'adoucir & de calmer les
" murmures des citoyens vexés. L'amour de la patrie, & la
" juftice due à tout citoyen qui la reclame ont nourri votre zéle.
" Elle s'eft rendue avec la même exactitude, vous n'avez jamais
" voulu faire vos répréfentations aux infractions faites à l'acte de
" ceffion, vous avez toujours craint d'autorifer une maffe de colo-

I   " nie

" ceſſion, and he diſcovered a ſentiment indiſpenſable in every
" governor who is deſirous of ſerving his king in the colonies:
" eſpecially as without inhabitants there can be no commerce, and
" without commerce few inhabitants. The proportion of induſtry
" to the bulk of the ſtate ſupports and props the throne. Liberty
" and emulation are the nurſing mothers of the ſtate; monopoly
" or excluſion, the tyrant and the ſtep-mother. Without liberty
" there are but few virtues. From deſpotiſm ſprings puſillanimity
" and the abyſs of vices. Man is conſidered as ſinning before God
" only becauſe he retains his free-will, upon which depends the
" liberty of inhabitants and merchants. Inſtances of protection
" and benevolence are converted into deſpotiſm: a ſingle authority
" would abſorb and annihilate every thing. All ranks, without
" diſtinction, can no longer, without running the riſk of being
" taxed with guilt, do any thing elſe but tremble, bow their necks
" to the yoke, and lick the duſt. The ſuperior council, bulwark
" of the tranquility of virtuous citizens, has ſupported itſelf only
" by the probity, the diſintereſtedneſs of merchants, and confidence
" of the united citizens in that tribunal. Without taking poſſeſ-
" ſion, without regiſtering, as was neceſſary, in the ſuperior coun-
" cil, titles and patents according to the laws, forms, and cuſtoms
" of the colony, and to the requiſition of the act of ceſſion, Mr.
" Ulloa has cauſed a preſident, three counſellors, and a ſecretary,
" nominated for the purpoſe, to take cognizance of facts which
" ſhould properly be determined by the ſuperior council, and in
" which French citizens were concerned. Often did diſcontents
" and diſguſts ſeem to force you to reſign your places, but you
" have always conſidered it as a duty of your ſtation of counſellors
" to the moſt chriſtian king, to alleviate and calm the murmurs
" of the oppreſſed citizens. The love of your country, and the
" juſtice due to every citizen who applies for it, have nouriſhed
" your zeal. It has been always rendered with the ſame exact-
" neſs; you never thought proper to make your repreſentations
" upon the act of ceſſion; you declined to authoriſe a numerous

diſ-

" nie mécontante & ménacée des plus grands malheurs, vous avez
" préféré la tranquilité publique : mais la maffe des habitans &
" negocians vous demandent juftice.

" Paffons à l'examen exaĉt & fcrupuleux des griefs, plaintes, &
" imputations contenues dans les repréfentations des habitans &
" des negocians. Quels triftes & notoires tableaux vous expofent
" les dites repréfentations ! les fleaux de la derniere guerre, une
" fufpenfion jufqu'à ce jour de payment de fept millions de papier
" du roi mis fur la place pour les befoins du fervice & reçus avec
" confiance par les negocians & habitans avoient reculé l'aifance &
" les facilités de la circulation ; mais l'aĉtivité & l'induftrie du cul-
" tivateur & negocians François avoient prefque furmonté les
" echecs. Les coins les plus reculés des poffeffions fauvages avoi-
" ent été découverts, le commerce des pelleteries étoit pouffé à fon
" plus haut point, la nouvelle culture du cotton adoptée, jointe
" aux indigots & tabacs, affuroient des chargemens aux armateurs.
" Le commiffaire de S. M. C. avoit annoncé & promis dix ans de
" liberté de commerce, ce tems fuffifoit pour tout citoyen François
" attaché à fon feigneur roi. Les tabacs de cette colonie prohibés
" en Efpagne, où ceux de la Havanne font les feuls permis : les
" bois (branche confiderable des revenus des habitans) inutiles à
" l'Efpagne fournis dans cet objet par fes poffeffions, & enfin
" l'indigo inférieur à celui de Guatimala qui en fournit plus qu'il
" n'en faut aux manufaĉtures d'Efpagne, rendoient ruineux les
" retours des denrées des habitans en Efpagne & livroient les dits
" habitans à la plus grande mifere. Le commiffaire de S. M. C.
" avoit conftaté publiquement l'impoffibilité du commerce de ce
" pays avec l'Efpagne : toute proteĉtion, faveur, encouragement,
" étoient journellement promis à l'habitant, le titre de proteĉteur
" fut

" difcontented colony, threatened with the moft dreadful cala-
" mities ; you preferred public tranquility : but the bulk of the
" inhabitants and merchants apply to you for juftice.

" Let us now proceed to an accurate and fcrupulous examina-
" tion of the grievances, complaints, and imputations contained
" in the reprefentations of the inhabitants and merchants. What
" fad and difmal pictures do the faid reprefentations bring before
" your eyes ! The fcourges of the laft war, a fufpenfion to this
" day of the payment of feven millions of paper-money of the
" king's, laid down to fupply the calls of the fervice, and received
" with confidence by the merchants and inhabitants, had ob-
" ftructed the eafe and facility of the circulation, but the activity
" and induftry of the planter and French merchants had almoft
" got the better of all difficulties. The moft remote corners of
" the poffeffions of the favages had been difcovered, the fur trade
" had been carried to its higheft perfection, the new culture of
" cotton adopted, thefe, joined to the indigoes and tobaccos, fecured
" cargoes to thofe who were concerned in fitting out fhips. His
" catholic majefty's commiffioner had promifed a free trade for
" ten years, that period being fufficient for every fubject of France
" attached to his fovereign the king. The tobaccos of this co-
" lony prohibited in Spain, or thofe of the Havannah, are the
" only ones allowed : the woods (a confiderable branch of the
" income of the inhabitants) being ufelefs to Spain, furnifhed in
" this article by its plantations, and the indigo being inferior to
" that of Guatimala, which fupplies more than requifite to the
" manufactures of Spain, thefe circumftances ruined the returns
" of the commodities of the inhabitants of this colony to Spain,
" and delivered up the faid inhabitants a prey to the moft dread-
" ful mifery. His catholic majefty's commiffioner had publickly
" proved the impoffibility of this country's trading with Spain :
" all patronage, favour, encouragement, were every day promifed
" the inhabitant ; the title of protector was decreed to Mr. Ulloa ;

2. "" fincerity,

" fut décerné à M. Ulloa, la bonne foi & la confiance nouriſſoient
" l'eſpérance & l'activité neceſſaire au cultivateur ; mais par quelle
" fatalité ruinante & imperceptible a-t-on vu une maiſon de vingt
" mille livres vendue ſix mille livres, & les habitations tout-à-coup
" perdre ſur leur valeur intrinſique la moitié & les deux tiers ? Les
" fortunes s'écroulent, & le numeraire eſt plus rare que jamais ;
" la confiance eſt perdue, & le decouragement eſt general, tout
" retentit du cri lugubre de la miſere, & le precieux titre de ci-
" toyen François ſe voit eclipſer, & le fatal décret conçernant le
" commerce de la Louiſiane porte le dernier coup de maſſue à
" l'anéantiſſement total de la colonie. Le pavillon Eſpagnol eſt
" arboré à la Baliſe & aux Illinois, & autres lieux, aucuns titres,
" aucunes patentes, n'ont été préſentées au conſeil ſupérieur : le
" tems fuit, les délais fixés pour la liberté de l'émigration ſe trou-
" veront expirés, la force tiraniſera, il faudra vivre aſſervis, chargés
" de chaines ou abandonner précipitamment des étabſiſſemens
" tranſportés du grand-pere au petit-fils. Tous les habitans &
" negocians vous demandent leur ſeigneur roi, Louis le bien-
" aimé ! leur fortunes & leur ſang ſont offert pour vivre & mourir
" François.

" Paſſons au réſumé des points de charge, griefs & imputations.
" M. Ulloa a fait juger par des conſeillers par lui nommés d'office
" des faits de la compétence du conſeil ſupérieur concernant les
" ſeuls citoyens François : les ſentences ont été ſignifiées & miſes
" à l'exécution contre les ſieurs Cadis & Leblanc ; M. Ulloa a
" ſoutenu les négres mecontens de leurs maitres, M. le commiſ-
" ſaire de S. M. C. n'a preſenté au conſeil ſupérieur aucun de ſes
" titres, pouvoirs, & proviſions, n'a point exhibé la copie de l'acte
" de ceſſion pour en demander acte, a ſans les dites formalités in-
" diſpenſables arboré pavillon Eſpagnol à la Baliſe, aux Illinois &
" autres lieux ; a, ſans autorité legale, puni & chatié & vexé des
citoyens

" fincerity and confidence nourifhed hope and the activity necef-
" fary to the planter : but by what undermining and imperceptible
" fatality have we feen a houfe worth twenty thoufand livres fold
" for fix thoufand, and habitations all on a fudden lofe one half
" and two-thirds of their intrinfic value ? Fortunes wafte away,
" and fpecie is more fcarce than ever ; confidence is loft, and the
" difcouragement becomes general ;- the plaintive cries of diftrefs
" are heard on every fide, the precious name of fubject of France
" is feen to be eclipfed, and the fatal decree concerning the com-
" merce of Louifiana gives the laft fatal ftroke to the colony,
" that muft totally annihilate it. The Spanifh ftandard is fet up
" at Balife and at the Illinois, and other places : no titles, no pa-
" tents were prefented to the fuperior council : time flies apace,
" the delays fixed for the liberty of emigration will foon expire,
" force will tyrannife, we muft live in flavery and loaded with
" chains, or precipitately forfake eftablifhments delivered down
" from the grandfather to the grandfon. All the inhabitants and
" merchants call upon you, their fovereign lord the king, Lewis
" the well-beloved; their treafures and their blood are offered,
" they are refolved to live and die French.

" Let us proceed to refume the points of the charge, grievances
" and imputations. Mr. Ulloa has caufed counfellors, named by
" himfelf, to take cognizance of facts, which fhould by right be
" determined by the fuperior council, relative to the fubjects of
" France alone : the fentences have been fignified and put in exe-
" cution againft meffieurs Cadis and Leblanc ; Mr. Ulloa has fup-
" ported the negroes, diffatisfied with their mafters; the commiffary
" of his catholic majefty has prefented to the fuperior council
" none of his titles, powers, and provifions ; has not exhibited a
" copy of the act of ceffion, in order to have it regiftered ; has
" without the faid indifpenfable formalities, fet up the Spanifh
" ftandard at Balife, at the Illinois, and other places ; has, with-
" out legal authority, punifhed and oppreffed fubjects of France ;

" has

" citoyens François ; en a même envoyé aux arrêts dans la fre-
" gate de S. M. C; a ufurpé, de fa feule autorité, le quart des
' communes des habitans de la ville, fe l'eft approprié & l'a fait
" entourer pour y faire paroitre fes-chevaux.

" Le tout murement examiné, je requiers pour le roi, que les
" fentences rendues par les confeillers nommés d'office & mifes à
" exécution contre les fieurs Cadis & Leblanc, citoyens François,
" foient declarés attentatoires à l'autorité de notre feigneur roi, &
" deftruétives du refpeét dû à fa juftice fouveraine féantes en fon
" confeil fupérieur, en ce qu'elles violent les loix, formes, & ufages
" de la colonie, confirmés & guarantis par l'aéte folemnel de cef-
" fion ; que M. Ulloa foit declaré infraétaire à nos loix, formes,
" ufages, & aux ordres de S. M. C. par l'aéte de ceffion & certifié
" par fa lettre dattée de la Havanne du dix Juillet 1765 ; qu'il foit
" déclaré ufurpateur d'une autorité illegale en faifant chatier &
" vexer des citoyens François fans avoir au préalable fatisfait aux
" loix, formes, & ufages de faire enrégiftrer au confeil fupérieur
" fes pouvoirs titres & provifions & la copie de l'aéte de ceffion
" pour en demander aéte ; qu'il foit enjoint à M. Ulloa commif-
" faire de S. M. C. de fortir de la colonie dans la fregate fur la-
" quelle il eft venu fous le plus court délai pour éviter des accidens
" ou de nouvelles rumeurs ; & d'aller rendre compte de fa conduite
" à S. M. C. & quant aux differens poftes établis par mon dit fieur
" Ulloa qu'il foit dit qu'il laiffera les ordres par écrit qu'il jugera
" convenable ; qu'il foit declaré refponfable de tous les evénemens
" qu'il auroit pû prevoir ; que meffieurs Aubry & Foucault foient
" priés & même fommés, au nom de notre feigneur roi, de conti-
" nuer à commander & regir la colonie comme ils faifoient ci-
" devant, que tous bâtimens fortant de cette colonie ne puiffent
être

" has even confined fome in the frigate of his catholic majefty;
" has by his authority alone ufurped the fourth part of the com-
" mon of the inhabitants of the city; has appropriated it to him-
" felf, and has caufed it to be furrounded, that his horfes might
" graze there.

" Having maturely weighed all this, I require, in behalf of the
" king, that the fentences pronounced by the counfellors nomi-
" nated for the purpofe, and put in execution againft meffieurs Cadi
" and Le Blanc, fubjects of France, be declared encroachments
" upon the authority of our fovereign lord the king, and deftruc-
" tive of the refpect due to his fupreme juftice, feated in his fu-
" perior council, inafmuch as they violate the laws, forms, and
" cuftoms of the colony, confirmed and guaranteed by the folemn
" act of ceffion; that Mr. Ulloa be declared to have violated our
" laws, forms, cuftoms, and the orders of his catholic majefty in
" the act of ceffion, which is confirmed by his letter from the
" Havannah, dated the 20th of July 1765; that he be declared
" ufurper of illegal authority, by caufing fubjects of France
" to be punifhed and oppreffed, without having previoufly com-
" plied with the laws, forms, and cuftoms, in caufing his powers,
" titles, and provifions to be regiftered in the fuperior council,
" with the copy of the act of ceffion; that it be enjoined Mr.
" Ulloa, commiffioner of his catholic majefty, to leave the
" colony in the frigate in which he came, without delay, to
" avoid accidents and new clamours, and to go and give an ac-
" count of his conduct to his catholic majefty : and with regard to
" the different pofts eftablifhed by the faid Mr. Ulloa, he is defired
" to leave in writing fuch orders, as he fhall think neceffary; that
" he be declared refponfible for all the events which he might
" have forefeen; that Meffrs. Aubry and Foucault be requefted,
" and even fummoned, in the name of our fovereign lord the
" king, to continue to command and govern the colony as they
" did heretofore; that fuch fhips as fail from this colony fhall not

N   be

" être expediés que fous des paffeports fignés de M. Foucault fai-
" fant fonctions d'ordonnateur ; que la prife de poffeffion ne
" pourra être propofée ni tentéc par aucuns moyens fans de nou-
" veaux ordres de S. M. T. C. que meffieurs Loyola, Gayarro, &
" Navarro feront declarés être garants de leur fignature dans les.
" bons qu'il font mis fur 'la place s'ils ne font apparoir des ordres
" de S. M. C. qui les ait autorifés à mettre les dits Bons & papiers
" fur la place ; qu'il leur foit accordé les delais néceffaires pour
" donner l'ordre qu'ils jugeront convenable à leur comptabilité.
" Que les habitans & negocians foient autorifés à choifir des dé-
" putés pour aller porter leurs fuppliques au feigneur roi ; qu'il foit
" fixé & arrêté, que le confeil fupérieur addreffera des repréfenta-
" tions à notre feigneur-roi, que l'arrêt à intervenir foit lû, publié,
" affiché, & enrégiftré ; que copies collationnées en foient envoyées
" à monfeigneur le duc de Praflin avec une lettre du confeil fupé-
" rieur & auffi dans les poftes de la colonie pour y être lues, pub-
" liées, affichées, & enrégiftrées."

Oui le rapport de meffieurs, M^{tre} Uchet écuyer, fieur de
Knion, & Piot Delaunay, confeillers commiffaires en cette partie,
le tout murement examiné & la matiere mife en délibération, le
procureur-général oui & retiré :

· Le confeil compofé de treize membres dont fix nommés. d'office;
ayant chacun donné fon avis par écrit, difant droit fur les dites
repréfentations, a declaré & déclare les fentences rendues par des
confeillers nommés d'office par M. Ulloa, & mifes à execution
contre les fieurs Cadis & Leblanc citoyens François, attentatoires
à l'autorité de notre feigneur roi & deftructives du refpeĉt du à fa
juftice fouveraine féante en fon confeil fupérieur ;. l'a declaré ufurpateur

" be difpatched without paffports figned by Mr. Foucault, in-
" vefted with the office of regulator, and difcharging the duties
" enjoined by it; that the taking poffeffion can neither be pro-
" pofed nor attempted by any means, without new orders being
" iffued by his moft chriftian majefty; that Meffrs. Loyala, Gayarro,
" and Navarro, fhall be declared guarantees of their fignature for
" the goods and paper-circulation which they have caufed to be ex-
" pofed in the market-place, if they do not produce the orders of
" his catholic majefty, empowering them to expofe the faid goods
" and paper-circulation in the public market-place; that a fufficient
" time be granted them to take the proper meafures to be ready to
" give an account of their proceedings. That the inhabitants and
" merchants be empowered to elect deputies to carry their petitions
" and fupplications to our fovereign lord the king; that it be fixed
" and determined, that the fuperior council fhall make reprefenta-
" tions to our fovereign lord the king; that the decree which
" is iffued fhall be read, fet up, publifhed, and regiftered; that
" confronted copies be fent to his grace the duke of Praflin, with
" a letter of the fuperior council, and likewife to the pofts of the
" colony, to be there read, fet up, publifhed, and regiftered."

The report being heard of Meffrs. Attre Ucbet, efq. le fieur de Knion,
and Piot Delaunay, counfellors and commiffioners appointed for this
purpofe, the whole being duly weighed and the fubject deliberated
upon, the attorney-general having been heard and having retired :

The council compofed of thirteen members, of which fix are
nominated to officiate, having each of them given their opinion in
writing, pronouncing upon the faid reprefentations, has declared
and declares the fentences pronounced by the counfellors nominated by Mr. Ulloa, and carried into execution againft Meffrs.
Cadis and Le Blanc, fubjects of France, to be encroachments upon
the authority of our fovereign lord the king, and deftructive of the
refpect due to his fupreme juftice, vefted in his fuperior council ;

has

pateur d'une autorité illegale en faifant chatier & vexer des citoyens François, fans avoir au préalable fatisfait aux loix & formes,
n'ayant fait apparoir ni enrégiftrer fes pouvoirs, titres & provifions;
& au préjudice des priviléges à eux confervés par le dit acte de
ceffion : & pour prévenir quelque violence du peuple, & éviter
quelque tumulte dangereux, le confeil par fa prudence ordinaire, fe
trouve obligé d'enjoindre, comme de fait il enjoint à M. Ulloa de
fortir de la colonie fous trois jours pour tout délai, foit dans la
fregate de S. M. C. fur laquelle il eft venu, ou dans tel autre bâtiment qui lui paroîtra convenable, & d'aller rendre compte de fa
conduite à S. M. C. a ordonné & ordonne que concernant les poftes
par lui établis dans le haut du fleuve, il laiffera tels ordres qu'il jugera convenables, le rendant refponfable de tous les evénemens qu'il
auroit pû prévoir. A prié & prie meffieurs Aubry & Foucault &
les fomme même au nom de notre feigneur roi, de continuer à
commander & regir, comme ils faifoient ci-devant la colonie : defend expreffement à tous armateurs & capitaines d'expédier aucun
bâtiment fous autre paffeport que celui de M. Foucault, faifant
fonction de l'ordonnateur : a ordonné & ordonne que là prife de
poffeffion pour S. M. C. ne pourra être propofée & tentée, par aucun moyens, fans des nouveaux ordres de S. M. T. C. qu'en confequence M. Ulloa s'embarquera fous le dit délai de trois jours
dans tel bâtiment qu'il jugera à propos avec tous les matelots qui
font à la Balife. Pour ce qui concerne meffieurs Loyola, Gayarro,
& Navarro, le confeil a ordonné qu'ils pourront refter pour fuivre
leur comptabilité jufques à de nouveaux ordres de S. M. T. C. en
par eux demeurer garaus de leurs fignatures dans les bons qu'ils ont
mis fur la place, à moins qu'ils ne faffent apparoir des ordres de
S. M. C. A autorifé & autorife les habitans & négocians, à choifir

telles

has declared and declares him an ufurper of illegal authority, in caufing fubjeᵈts of France to be punifhed and oppreffed without having previoufly complied with the 'laws and forms, having neither produced his powers, titles, and provifions, nor caufed them to be regiftered, and that in prejudice of the privileges infured to them by the faid aᵈt of ceffion : and to prevent any violence of the populace, and avoid any dangerous tumult, the council, in its ufual prudence, finds itfelf obliged to enjoin, as in faᵈt it enjoins, Mr. Ulloa to quit the colony, allowing him only the fpace of three days, either in the frigate of his catholic majefty, in which he came, or in whatever veffel he fhall think proper, and go and give an account of his conduᵈt to his catholic majefty : it has likewife ordained and ordains, that with regard to the pofts eftablifhed by him at the upper part of the river, he fhall leave fuch orders as he judges expedient, making him at the fame time refponfible for all the events which he might have forefeen. It has likewife requefted and requefts Meffrs. Aubry and Foucault, and even cites them in the name of our fovereign lord the king, to continue to command and govern the colony as they did heretofore : at the fame time exprefsly forbids all thofe who fit out veffels, and all captains of fhips, to difpatch any veffel with any other paffport but that of Mr. Foucault, who is to do the office of regulator : has likewife ordered and orders, that the taking poffeffion for his catholic majefty can neither be propofed nor attempted by any means without new orders from his moft chriftian majefty : that in confequence Mr. Ulloa fhall embark in the fpace of three days in whatever fhip he fhall think proper. With regard to what relates to Meffrs. Loyola, Gayarro, and Navarro, the counfel has decreed that they may ftay and follow their refpeᵈtive bufinefs, till they have received new orders from the moft chriftian king, and remain fureties of their fignatures for the goods and paper-circulation which they expofed to public view in the market-place, except they produce the orders of his catholic majefty. Has likewife authorifed and authorifes the

inhabitants

telles perfonnes qu'ils croiront convenable pour aller porter leur fupplique au feigneur roi, & a arrêté que pareillement le confeil fupérieur addreffera des repréfentations à notre dit feigneur roi ; ordonne que le préfent arrêt fera imprimé, lû, publié & affiché & enregiftré en tous les lieux & poftes de cette colonie, & que copie en fera envoyée à Mgr. le duc de Praflin, miniftre de la marine.

Mandons, à tous nos huiffiers ou fergents fur ce requis, faire pour l'exécution du préfent tous actes & exploits neceffaires, de ce faire donnons pouvoir. Et enjoignons au fubftitut du procureur géneral du roi, tenir le main à l'exécution, & d'en avertir la cour en fon tems.

Donné, en la chambre de confeil, le vingt neuf Octobre 1768.

Par le confeil,

G A R I C, greffier en chef.

Je protefte contre l'arrêt du confeil, qui renvoye monfieur Don Antonio de Ulloa de cette colonie ; leurs majeftés trés chrétienne & catholique feront offenfés du traitement que l'on fait éprouver à une perfonne de fon caractere, & malgré le peu de forcés qui j'ai fous mes ordres, je m'oppoferois de tout mon pouvoir à fon départ, fi je ne craignois que fa vie ne fût expofée, aufli bien que celle de tous les Efpagnols qui fe trouvent ici.

Délibéré à la chambre de confeil, ce 29 Octobre 1768.

Signé

A U B R Y.

Colla-

inhabitants and merchants to chufe whatever perfons they think proper to go with their petition to our fovereign lord the king, and has decreed that the fuperior council fhall in like manner make reprefentations to our faid fovereign lord the king : orders that the prefent decree fhall be printed, read, fet up, publifhed, and regiftered in all places and pofts of this colony, and that a copy of it fhall be fent to his grace the duke of Praflin, minifter of the marine.

We order all our bailiffs and ferjeants to perform all the acts and ceremonies requifite for carrying the prefent decree into execution ; we at the fame time empower them to do fo. We alfo enjoin the fubftitute of the king's attorney-general to fuperintend the execution, and to apprize the court at a proper time.

Given at the council-chamber on the 29th of October, 1768.

By the council,

G A R I C, principal fecretary.

I proteft againft the decree of the council, which difmiffes don Antonio de Ulloa from this colony ; their moft chriftian and catholic majefties will be offended at this ufage of a perfon of his character ; and tho' I have fo fmall a force fubject to my orders, I fhould with all my might oppofe his departure, were I not apprehenfive of endangering his life, as well as the lives of all the Spaniards in this country.

Deliberated at the council-chamber this 29th of October 1768.

Signed

A U B R Y.

Con-

Collationé, fur l'original demeuré és minutes de greffe, par nous greffier en chef fouffigné, à la Nouvelle Orléans le deux Novembre 1768.

G A R I C, greffier en chef.

EXTRAIT

Compared with the original, left amongſt the minutes of the ſecretary's office, by me, the firſt ſecretary, whoſe name is hereto ſigned, at New Orleans, 2d of November 1768.

GARIC, principal ſecretary.

EXTRACT

EXTRAIT des REGISTRES du CONSEIL SUPERIEUR de la PROVINCE de la LOUISIANE, du 31 Octobre 1768.

Vu par le conseil supérieur, la protestation faite par M. Aubry, chevalier de l'ordre royal & militaire de St. Louis, commandant pour sa majesté-très-chretienne de la ditte province, à l'arrêt de la cour rendu le 29 du present mois, contre M. Ulloa commissaire de S. M. C. icelle lue l'audience tenante ; oui sur ce, le procureur-général du roi en ses conclusions ; la matiere mise en deliberations : le conseil, sans condamner les motifs qui ont donné lieu à M. Aubry, de protester contre l'arrêt de la cour du 29 du présent, a declaré & declare la ditte protestation nulle, & comme non avenue ; ordonne que le dit arrêt sortira son plein & entier effet, ce qui sera exécuté en toute sa forme & teneur.

Donné & delibéré en la chambre de conseil, le 31 Octobre 1768.

Par le conseil,

GARIC, greffier en chef.

F I N.

EXTRACT of the REGISTERS of the SUPERIOR COUNCIL of the PROVINCE of LOUISIANA, 31ſt October 1768.

The ſuperior council having taken into conſideration the proteſt made by Mr. Aubry, knight of the royal and military order of St. Louis, governor of ſaid province for his moſt chriſtian majeſty, againſt the decree of court delivered on the 29th of the preſent month againſt Mr. Ulloa, commiſſioner of his catholic majeſty; and this proteſt being read whilſt the audience was holding, and the king's attorney-general being heard thereupon, and the matter thoroughly debated ; the council, without condemning the motives which have cauſed Mr. Aubry to proteſt againſt the decree of court of the 29th of the preſent month, has declared and declares the ſaid proteſt null and void, and orders that the ſaid decree ſhall have its entire effect, which ſhall be executed in its full force and tenor.

Given and reſolved at the council-chamber, October 31, 1768.

By the council,

G A R I C, principal ſecretary.

F I N I S.

Lightning Source UK Ltd.
Milton Keynes UK
UKHW020339081118
331957UK00008B/355/P